THE GREAT BETRAYAL

ROBERT CALABRO

Copyright © 2017 Robert Calabro.

All rights reserved. No part of this book may be reproduced, stored, or transmitted by any means—whether auditory, graphic, mechanical, or electronic—without written permission of both publisher and author, except in the case of brief excerpts used in critical articles and reviews. Unauthorized reproduction of any part of this work is illegal and is punishable by law.

ISBN: 978-1-4834-6387-2 (sc)
ISBN: 978-1-4834-6386-5 (e)

Library of Congress Control Number: 2017900020

Because of the dynamic nature of the Internet, any web addresses or links contained in this book may have changed since publication and may no longer be valid. The views expressed in this work are solely those of the author and do not necessarily reflect the views of the publisher, and the publisher hereby disclaims any responsibility for them.

Any people depicted in stock imagery provided by Thinkstock are models, and such images are being used for illustrative purposes only.
Certain stock imagery © Thinkstock.

Lulu Publishing Services rev. date: 01/30/2017

To my loving wife, Maryann, my two sons,

Robert and Christopher, their families, and our extended families.

Chapter 1

A NEW COUNTRY IS BORN

In 1781, Congress, under the Articles of Confederation, created the first national bank. This bank superseded all of the banks located in the thirteen colonies. Created to help finance our war of independence, this bank was granted a monopoly on the issuing of bills of credit on a national level.

Robert Morris was the head of the first national bank.

After the war, a number of state banks were chartered, including, in 1784, the Bank of New York and the Bank of Massachusetts.

In the last decade of the 1700s, we had only three banks, but we used various coinages, which included but were not limited to Spanish, English, French, and Portuguese coins and scrip. Scrip was a term used for paper money in the 1700s. The values of the coins fluctuated geographically, but this was irrelevant in a country dominated by local trading.

Supporters of the bank argued that if the nation were to grow and to prosper, it needed a universally accepted, standard coinage, and this would best be provided by the US Mint, aided and supported by a national bank and an excise tax. Opponents of the bank argued that government monopolization of money was a corrupt exercise that would impoverish the people.

In 1791, Congress chartered the First Bank of the United States, a nationwide commercial bank that was jointly owned by the federal government and private stockholders, that served as the bank for the federal government, and that operated as a regular commercial bank, acting in competition with state banks. When depositors brought state bank notes to First Bank of the United States, it would present these notes to the state banks, demanding gold, which hampered the state banks' ability to issue notes and maintain adequate reserves. When the charter of the First Bank of the United States came up for renewal, it was opposed by the states. The renewal of the charter did not pass Congress.

The Second Bank of the United States opened in January of 1817 to help finance the War of 1812.

The charter of the Second Bank of the United States was for twenty years and, therefore, up for renewal in 1836. President Andrew Jackson was president at the time. President Jackson was opposed to the idea of a central bank that was named "Bank of America." He believed that bestowing power and responsibility upon a single bank was the cause of inflation and other perceived evils. He vetoed the renewal legislation. His veto was sustained by one vote.

1837–1863: "Free Banking Era"

Prior to 1837 a bank charter could be obtained only by a specific legislative act, but in 1837, the Michigan Act allowed for the automatic chartering of banks without legislative approval. The following year, New York enacted similar legislation with the Free Banking Act, and other states soon followed. These banks could issue bank notes against gold and silver that they held in reserve. During this era the lending standards were relaxed as well as a lack of regulation. The states learned from their mistakes and passed the necessary corrective legislation.

Congress passed the National Bank Act in order to retire the greenback, which was paper money not backed by gold. We went off the gold standard during the Civil War. During the period of the Civil War, we had high inflation due to a lack of monetary discipline.

The panic of 1893 caused a severe nationwide depression. The issue of money was the main issue. The Silverites, led by the Democratic nominee, William Jennings Bryan, called for the issue of silver coins only. He argued that the issuing of silver coins would mean that the money supply would be inflated, which meant more money for everyone.

The Republican nominee was William McKinley, who argued that the gold standard, which is sound money, would provide monetary discipline would restore prosperity.

The Panic of 1907 and the Pujo Committee

The Pujo Committee report concluded that a community of influential financial leaders led by J. P. Morgan had gained control of major manufacturing, transportation, mining, communications, and financial markets of the United States.

The Pujo report singled out the culprits, including Paul Warburg, Jacob H. Schiff, Felix M. Warburg, Frank E. Peabody, William Rockefeller, and Benjamin Strong Jr. The report identified over $22 billion in resources and capitalization controlled by J. P. Morgan and his associates.

The committee investigation inspired public support for ratification of the Sixteenth Amendment in 1913, passage of the Federal Reserve Act that same year, and the passage of the Clayton Antitrust Act in 1914.

Abandonment of the Gold Standard

In order to deal with deflation that started after the stock market crash of 1929, President Roosevelt took us off the gold standard. At the time, the dollar price of gold was $20.67 per ounce. On April 5, 1933, President Roosevelt issued Executive Order 6102, which compelled every American to turn over his or her gold to the government. Those who did so were compensated at $20.67 per ounce. Six weeks later, President Roosevelt devalued the dollar by increasing the gold price to $35 per ounce. This resulted in a loss of purchasing power for the dollar. When currencies are devalued, the devaluation is subtracted from purchasing power. This is the hidden tax that is known as "inflation."

The Trading with the Enemy Act of 1917 was used as a justification for gold confiscation.

This act had originally been intended to criminalize economic relationships between declared enemies of the United States. One provision of the act granted the president the power to regulate and even prohibit, under such rules and regulations as he may prescribe, any transactions in foreign exchange, export, or earmarking of gold or silver coin or bullion or currency by any person within the United States. In 1918 the act was amended to extend its provisions two years beyond the conclusion of hostilities and to allow the president to investigate, regulate, or prohibit even the hoarding of gold by an American.

As amended by the emergency Banking act of 1933, the Trading with the Enemy Act no longer said that simply during time of war could the president prohibit the export of gold or take action against banking. Now these actions could be taken during time of war or during any other period of national emergency declared by the president. In order to protect the wealth of the American people who own gold, this act should be repealed.

Glass Steagall Act of 1933: The Glass-Steagall Act of 1933 was passed in reaction to the collapse of a large portion of the American commercial banking system in early 1933. The purpose of the Glass-Steagall Act was to separate commercial banking from investment banking.

On November 12, 1999, Glass-Steagall was repealed by the passage of the Gramm-Leach-Bliley Act. The repeal of the Glass Steagall Act of 1933 effectively removed the separation that had previously existed between Wall Street investment banks and depositary banks. This repeal was one of the root causes of the 2008 recession.

Since 2009, the commercial banks have grown by 25 percent. Derivative trading has increased dramatically. Fifty percent of the nation's assets are concentrated in five banks. This is not risk management; this is insanity. As previously mentioned, I was in the insurance business for forty years. One of the first things you learn in the insurance business is to identify your loss exposures. Our biggest loss exposure is a collapse of the fiat monetary system. In order to mitigate the next financial crisis, the banks must be broken up into smaller units. We need Glass-Steagall 2.

Credit Unions: The first credit union in the United States was established in 1908 in New Hampshire. At the time, banks were unwilling to lend to many poor laborers, who then turned to corrupt moneylenders and loan sharks. Businessman Edward Filene spearheaded an effort to secure legislation for credit unions for the purpose of loaning money to the working poor and middle class.

McFadden Act: The McFadden Act was enacted in 1927 based on recommendations made by the comptroller of the currency, Henry May Dawes. The act sought to give national banks competitive equality with state-chartered banks by letting national banks branch to the extent permitted by state law.

Savings and loan associations: The savings and loan associations were created in the early twentieth century for the purpose of providing mortgages to the working poor and middle class. They also provided passbook savings accounts.

We were taught that banks loan out deposits and are able to loan out up to 90 percent of deposits. They must keep 10 percent of their deposits in reserve at all times.

The truth of the matter is that loans create deposits. As banks make loans, they simultaneously create both the loan and the deposit. Say the banking system makes $1 billion in deposits as it credits the borrowers' accounts. There is no need to have deposits ahead of time. This is why lending is called credit creation. The deposits come from nowhere. With a few keystrokes, the banking system creates money. The banking system creates reserves. This is the amount they have to set aside against those deposits. We have a fractional-reserve banking system. All banks are required by law to set aside 10 percent of their deposits to cover withdrawals. These deposits are held by the twelve Federal Reserve banks. The banks cannot lend out reserves. On a system-wide basis, there is nothing the banks can do to lower reserves. The central bank determines the level of reserves through its actions. So if the bank cannot lend out reserves, what was the purpose of quantitative easing?

Former banker and now investment advisor Chris Mayer wrote in an article for Agora Financial in December, 2013 which stated that "Because QE drives down interest rates, The lower rates may, at the margin, bring in borrowers who might not have otherwise borrowed. They may induce lenders to make loans they otherwise would not have made. But the connection is far weaker than most people think. And it has nothing to with reserves. If banks do not see a way to make a profit by lending they will not lend. I can tell you when I was in banking, we never made a loan based on what our reserve position was.

What the Fed's manipulating of interest did was to set off a boom in so-called risk assets like stocks. Lower interest rates put pressure on asset prices.

You can criticize QE for inflating asset prices by keeping rates lower than they otherwise might be. (And it clearly helps borrowers and punishes savers.)"

On December 23, 1913, President Wilson signed the Aldrich-Vreeland Act, creating our countries third central bank, called the Federal Reserve. The Federal Reserve's primary mission is stabilize prices and to control inflation. They have failed! Since the Fed opened for business on January 1, 1914, we have lost approximately 90 percent of our purchasing power. Inflation on a cumulative basis is 2,200 percent!

The Federal Reserve system is a combination of private and public elements. The Fed is headed by a chairperson who is nominated by the president and subject to Senate confirmation. The vice chair is also nominated by the president and subject to confirmation by the Senate. The Fed also has seven board of governors who are nominated by the president, subject to

Senate confirmation and serve for fourteen-year terms. They are based in Washington, DC.

The twelve regional banks are located in our major cities and are privately owned by the commercial banks in each region. Those private stockholders elect a board of directors, and the directors hire a president for each regional bank. They are supervised by the board of governors.

Interest rate policy is not made by the governors alone or by the reserve bank presidents. Interest rate policy is set by the Federal Open Market Committee, the FOMC.

The FOMC meets eight times per year, every six weeks. It has twelve members consisting of all seven members of the board of governors, plus five of the twelve regional reserve bank presidents. Of the five regional reserve bank presidents who can vote on the FOMC, one has a permanent seat. That is the president of the Federal Reserve Bank of New York. The other four rotate from among the remaining eleven regional banks on a one-year term. This rotation is important because some of the regional reserve banks presidents are "hawks" (favoring rate hikes). Some others are "doves" (favoring continuing easing of interest rates). Knowing which are on the FOMC each year is part of what you need to know to forecast policy.

The Federal Reserve conducts what are known as "open market operations." When the Fed wants to print money, they buy government-debt securities, Treasury bills, bonds and notes, and other debt instruments. This is done through dealers, who are the big commercial banks. With a few strokes of the mouse, money is created from nothing. The dealer deducts his or her commission, and the money is sent to the former owner of the security. This is the way the money supply is expanded. When the Fed wants to contract the money supply, they sell their securities through a dealer, who in turn creates a market for the security. The money that the Fed receives is supposed to be taken out of circulation. What does happen, more often than not, is that the money is sent to the Treasury. Open market operations are conducted by the Federal Bank of New York. Part of our gold stock is contained at the Federal Bank of New York, as well as Fort Knox and West Point.

In his farewell address to the nation, President Wilson apologized to the nation for signing the Aldrich-Vreeland Act. He stated the following:

> I am a most unhappy man. I have unwittingly ruined my country. A great industrial nation is controlled by its system of credit. Our system of credit is concentrated. The growth of the nation, therefore, and all our activities are in the hands of a few men.
>
> We have come to be one of the worst ruled, one of the most complete controlled and dominated governments in the civilized world. No longer a government by conviction and the vote of the majority, but a government by the opinion and duress of a small group of dominant men.

In 1933, President Franklin Delano Roosevelt closed the countries banks so that emergency legislation could be passed. Congress passed the Emergency Banking Act, which provided for a system of reopening sound banks under Treasury supervision, with federal loans available when needed. Three-quarters of the banks in the Federal System reopened within the next three days. Billions of dollars in hoarded currency and gold flowed back into them within a month, thus stabilizing the banking system. By the end of 1933, 4,004 small, local banks were permanently closed and merged into larger banks. The depositors of these banks eventually received eighty-six cents on the dollar of their deposits.

In June of 1933, Congress created the Federal Deposit Insurance Corporation (FDIC), which insured deposits for up to $2,500 beginning on January 1, 1934. Savings deposits are now insured for $250,000.

Bretton Woods System: On July 1, 1944, the Bretton Woods Conference was held at the Mount Washington Hotel in Bretton Woods, New Hampshire, where delegates from forty-four countries created a new international monetary system known as the "Bretton Woods system."

Under this system, the dollar was designated as the world's reserve currency. This meant that all international transactions were to be done in dollars. The dollar would still be backed by gold. In order to participate in the international markets, all participating countries had to hold dollars in reserve. In order to accomplish this, the United States had to issue more treasury bills, bonds, and notes. When our debt securities held by the countries that purchased them matured, we sent them cash. The more debt securities we issued, the more debt we incurred. In exchange for this privilege, we agreed to redeem any countries dollar reserves with gold at $35 per ounce.

John Maynard Keynes represented Britain at the Bretton Woods Conference. At the conference, he lobbied for three things: the world bank, which would be used to loan money for developing nations; the International Monetary Fund, which would serve as a central bank for the world in the event of a world financial crisis and also advocated a one-world currency, called the "bancor", which would be backed by a basket of commodities, with gold holding the highest percentage. What he envisioned was a one-world government, with a one-world currency. John Maynard Keynes was a British socialist. He belonged to the Fabian Society. The mascot of the Fabian Society is a wolf in sheep's clothing. This proposal was rejected by the finance ministers of the world. I will explain the Keynesian theory of economics in chapter 5.

In an article written in *National Review* in December 2008, Dr. Lewis Lehrman and John Mueller wrote an article titled "Go Forward to Gold: How to Lift the Reserve Currency Curse." They asserted,

> Official reserves are money held by governments and central banks for the settlement of international payments. An official reserve currency is one everybody agrees to accept and right now that currency is the dollar. But foreign exchange reserves are commonly held in the form of government debts of the nation that issued the currency. In the case of the US, that includes all those government bonds piling up in China and else ware. The problem

> is that, unlike gold, official dollar reserves increase the money supply in one country without decreasing it in the other. When reserves are being increased, the effect is inflation. When reserves are liquidated, the effect is deflation, potentially dangerous deflation.
>
> The key difference between a reserve currency system and the gold standard is that foreign exchange reserves, in the form of government bonds, are not only assets of the national authority that holds them, as gold was; they are also, unlike gold debts of the country that issues them. Thus, when foreign monetary authorities acquire US debt securities as reserves, US monetary authorities are, in effect, borrowing the same amount.

This is part of the reason why we have incurred, to date, twenty trillion dollars in debt that will probably never be paid. Dr. Lehrman and Mr. Mueller also wrote,

> To understand how the dollar's reserve-currency role helped cause the recent bubbles and the ensuing crisis in the world financial system, we must apply the analysis of the great French economist and central banker Jacques Rueff, who was the first to explain this process. As a financial attaché in London in the early 1930s, Rueff witnessed the collapse of the post-World War1 monetary system. He correctly diagnosed the stock market boom of the 1920s, and the subsequent crash and price deflation, as a result of massive official accumulation and subsequent liquidation of foreign-exchange reserves. Foreign countries dollar reserves were certainly not the only factor involved, but before and during the depression they were large enough to play a decisive role.

In his book *Pillars of Prosperity*, Dr. Ron Paul documented that from 1944 to 1971 (a period of twenty-seven years), a total of 409 million ounces of gold left our shores due to currency redemptions for gold at $35 per ounce. The first redemption occurred in 1965, when President De Gaulle of France redeemed $150 million for gold at $35 per ounce. Spain redeemed $60 million of gold at $35 per ounce. The straw that broke the camel's back was when Britain wanted to redeem $3 billion for gold at $35 an ounce. President Nixon and Secretary Connelly refused. They were afraid of a continual run on gold. President Nixon blamed the suspension of the gold standard on speculators. Nothing could be further from the truth. The problem at the time was monetary ease and large budget deficits. The Bretton Woods system, as Dr. Lehrman and John Mueller have pointed out, was flawed from the very beginning. The suspension of the gold standard (also known as the "Nixon shock") occurred on August 15, 1971. Our mistake, which we have yet to correct, was not going back to the classical gold standard after World War I.

Deregulation of the 1980s and 1990s

In 1982, Congress passed the Depository Institutions Act. This act significantly reduced the differences between banks and other financial institutions. This act is also referred to as "deregulation." This act called for the reduction of loan standards, which resulted in the closing of over 500 savings and loan institutions, from 1980 to 1988. By reducing loan underwriting standards, the moral hazard increased. There always was and always will be a moral hazard in finance. This is a lesson that we have yet to learn. The reason why we do not learn from our mistakes is arrogance and politics.

Savings and loan crisis: The savings and crisis of the 1980s and 1990s resulted in a failure of 747 out of the 3,234 savings and loan associations in the United States. As of December 31,1995, the government estimated that the total cost for resolving the 747 failed institutions was $87.9 billion.

Late-2000s financial crisis: The financial crisis of 2008 was the worst crisis since the depression of 1929. The housing bubble burst because of a relaxation of lending standards. The culprits were the politicians who forced Fannie Mae and Freddie Mac to reduce lending standards. The requirement for a 20 percent down payment on a home was reduced. We all observed advertisements on TV that you could purchase a home with no money down. The people who were the most vulnerable were the uneducated working poor and middle class. They were set up to fail. It was the lobbyists who lobbied Congress for the reduction of lending standards so as to enrich themselves with increased revenue.

In his book *The Great Deformation*, the distinguished David Stockman stated,

> The preponderant reality of contemporary governance is money-based interest group politics. Accordingly, if a class of citizen's merits income transfers from the state under some imaginable public policy standard, the worst possible answer is to shower a random subset of that class with in kind subsidies through the private market.
>
> These in kind subsidies almost always get captured by vendors and providers; they become the sustenance for yet another syndicate of crony capitalist rent-seekers. The better answer is to impose a means test and mail cash to eligible citizens. In the case at hand, such cash transfers would allow beneficiaries to choose between applying the cash to rent, a mortgage, or something else.

The financial-shock recession ended in 2009. Although many opinions have been rendered as to the cause of the financial crisis, the US Senate issued the Levin-Coburn Report, which found "that the crisis was not a natural disaster, but the result of high-risk, complex financial products; undisclosed conflicts of interest; and the failure of regulators, the credit agencies, and the market itself to rein in the excesses of Wall Street."

Congress passed the Dodd-Frank Wall Street Reform and Consumer Protection Act after the crisis of 2008. This law is the most comprehensive financial law passed since the depression of 1929.

The Volcker Rule is part of the Dodd-Frank Wall Street Reform and Consumer Protection Act. The Volcker Rule does allow banks to continue market making, underwriting, hedging, trading of government securities, offering hedge funds and private equity funds, and acting as agents, brokers, and custodians. Banks cannot engage in these activities if doing so would create a material conflict of interest, expose the bank to high-risk assets or trading strategies, or generate instability within the bank or within the overall US financial system. It is a shame, that no questions were asked about this important part of the law during the Presidential debates of 2016.

Some of our fellow citizens have criticized this law as being too overbearing. Banks are also required to comply with the Basel I–III suggested regulations that were written by the Bank of International Settlements located in Basel, Switzerland.

In order not to overburden the banks with excessive regulations, the next president should form a committee of trustworthy financial experts and make a determination as to whether or not the banks are overregulated. What we the people must always bear in mind is that regulations are hidden taxes. The cost of complying with regulations is always passed on to the consumer.

Chapter 2

THE FAILURE AND EVIL OF FIAT MONEY

Fiat money is paper money without precious-metal backing that people are required by law to accept. It allows politicians to increase spending without raising taxes. Fiat money is the cause of inflation, and the amount by which people lose purchasing power is exactly the amount that was taken from them and transferred to their government by this process. Inflation is therefore a hidden tax. This tax is the most unfair of all because it falls most heavily on those who have the least ability to pay. It punishes the thrifty by eroding the value of their savings. This creates resentment among the people, leading to political unrest and national disunity.

A nation that resorts to fiat money has doomed itself to economic hardship and national disunity.

In this chapter, I will give you an overview of the number of times fiat currencies have failed in the twentieth century.

Currency Crisis 1: 1921–1936: It begins in Germany's epic devaluation of the reichsmark. Germany was assessed $30 billion in reparations as a result of the Treaty of Versailles. The leaders of the Weimer Republic panicked, and the politicians pressured the Central Bank to engage in currency devaluation, which eventually destroyed the reichsmark. Currency devaluation brings out the worst in all of us. The devaluation of a nation's currency falls the hardest on the working poor and middle class. All nations were forced to devalue their currencies in order to protect their exports. In 1933, President Roosevelt devalued the dollar from $20.67 per ounce to $35 per ounce. The currency crisis ended in 1936 with an agreement between the United States, Britain, France and Germany. The Weimar Republic was overthrown by the Nazis as the first currency crisis came to an end. World War II started in 1939 when Germany invaded Poland. Currency wars and trade wars are zero-sum games. No one wins. The end result is resentment that builds between nations, which comes to a head and a real war starts, as in World War II.

Currency Crisis 2, 1967–1987: There were events that occurred prior to the second currency war. President Johnson won the presidency in a landslide. President Johnson instituted what was known as "guns and butter." Acting on the Gulf of Tonkin Resolution he escalated the war in Vietnam in 1965, the same year that President de Gaulle of France redeemed $150 million of gold at $35 an ounce as previously mentioned. Spain made a redemption worth $60 million. President de Gaulle was angered by the Bretton Woods arrangement and temporarily withdrew from the military part of NATO. This was not a good year for America.

In 1968, President Johnson asked Congress not to back any new printed money with gold. He knew that he would not be able to expand the war in Vietnam, have the Great Society programs, and live within gold-standard discipline at the same time. The real costs of Vietnam and the Great Society have now become apparent. President Johnson signed the Kennedy tax cuts into law, which gave a boost to the economy. We grew by over 5 percent in the first year that the tax cuts were implemented. Growth averaged over 4.8 percent annually during the Kennedy/Johnson years. But almost from the start, inflation occurred because of the excessive amount of spending on the war and the Great Society. In measuring inflation on a yearly basis, it went from 1.9 percent in 1965 to 3.5 percent in 1966. The initial perception on the part of the government was that prices were going up. What was really happening was that the currency was going down. Higher prices are just a symptom of currency collapse.

In one of his writings, author James Rickards stated the following:

> Britain fired the first salvo. A sterling crisis had been brewing since 1964 and came to a boil in 1967. The British devalued the pound sterling from 2.80 to 2.40 a 14.3 percent devaluation. In 1945, UK pound sterling comprised a larger percentage of global reserves, the combined holdings of all central banks than the dollar. This position deteriorated steadily, and by 1965 26 percent of global reserves were in sterling. The British balance of payments had been deteriorating since the early 1960s. They grew sharply in 1964. The straw that probably broke the camel's back was the six-day war in 1967 when the Suez Canal was closed. The Smithsonian agreement, the plaza accord and the Louvre accords attempted to stabilize the system. The currency war ended in 1987.

Currency Crisis 3, 2010–present: It began with President Obama announcing plans to double US exports in five years. The only way to achieve this goal was to devalue the currency. Months later, the Brazilian finance minister declared, "We are in the midst of an international currency war." Other countries have begun to devalue their currencies against our dollar. There have been events subsequent to the start of the third currency war that do not bode well for the dollar.

China has signed international currency agreements with Germany, Brazil, Russia, Australia, Japan, the United Arab Emirates, India, and South Africa. Japan and India also recently signed a currency deal linking their currencies closer together and lessening their dependency on US dollars.

In a report, Robert Fisk wrote, "In the most profound financial change in recent Middle East history, Gulf Arabs are planning—along with China, Russia, Japan, and France—to end dollar dealing for oil, moving instead to a basket of currencies including the Japanese yen and Chinese yuan, the euro, gold and a new unified currency planned for nations in the Gulf

Cooperation Council, including Saudi Arabia, Abu Dhabi, Kuwait, and Qatar."

The IMF has proposed replacing the dollar with their currency, called Special Drawing Rights, or SDRs, which represent special claims on the currencies of the IMF members. SDRs were created in 1969 and can be converted into any one currency based on a weighted basket of international currencies. When the IMF lends money, it typically does so with SDRs. The IMF also proposed creating SDR-Denominated Bonds, which could reduce central banks dependence on US Treasury bonds. The fund also suggested that certain assets, such as oil and gold, that are traded in US dollars could be prices in SDRs. This does not bode well for the dollar. Our reserve currency days are numbered!

In the 1990s there was a crisis with the Mexican peso that led to Mexican devaluation. The cause excessive money-printing/credit expansion. Three times in the twentieth century, the Argentine peso collapsed because of devaluation and excessive money printing. Prior to Juan Peron taking office, Argentina was listed in the top-ten growth economies in the world. Argentina had the second-largest gold reserves in the world after the United States. Juan Peron, who was influenced by Benito Mussolini of Italy, sold all of the country's gold. This wrongheaded decision led to hyperinflation in Argentina for many years. In 2001 Argentina defaulted on its sovereign debt, which amounted to $100 billion, a world record. Hopefully with a new administration in power, Argentina will finally recover.

There was a currency crisis that originated in Thailand in 1997/98. At the time, US interest rates were going up. People borrowed dollars and invested in Thailand's markets. There were projects like golf courses, hotels, restaurants, etc. Thailand, as well as other Southeast Asia countries, pegged their currencies to the dollar. If you invested in dollars, people were told that the Thai baht would have the same value as the US dollar. Investors were attracted since there was no currency-exchange risk. Investors could borrow cheap money, put it to work in a faster-growing market, and make a lot of money. As interest rates in the United States went up, there was a capital flight out of Thailand and Indonesia as well. This meant that

Thailand had to sell dollars from their reserves and bought baht in order to maintain the peg. It was apparent that the Thai central bank could continue selling dollars and buying their own currency. The demand for getting dollars out of Thailand was so great that it began to overwhelm their reserves. Finally, Thailand broke the link to the dollar. Then they devalued their currency, which meant that investors could still get dollars but fewer of them for each baht. That started a panic, and everyone wanted to get out of Thailand. This crisis caused sovereign-wealth-investment firm, Long-Term Capital Management, to nearly default. James Rickards, the author of *Currency Wars* and *The Death of Money*, negotiated a bailout with the Fed. This crisis caused Russia to default on its sovereign debt.

In the early part of 2016, the IMF negotiated what is called the "Shanghai accord" between the United States, China, Japan, and Europe. Because of the previous crisis in China, the IMF suggested that Europe and Japan keep their currencies stronger than the dollar and the yuan. They deemed it important that China keep their peg with the dollar. This would help China in the short term with regard to keeping their exports competitive. There is another negative aspect of currency devaluation. When currency devaluation is done, not only is purchasing power reduced, but also the country doing the devaluation is importing inflation. This is due to the fact that since the local currency is purchasing less, it makes imports from other countries more expensive.

China is the largest gold producer in the world. They are openly and secretly buying as much gold as possible. Their purpose is to have a seat at the table at the IMF. The IMF currency, SDRs, is backed by nothing. The dollar, British pound, euro, and Japanese yen are used to calculate the value of the SDR. China wants a seat at the table, and someday they want to be the world's reserve currency. This is a long way off, since China does not have a mature bond market. In order to be a reserve currency, you have to make your currency available for purchase.

The amount of gold that China now has is approximately four thousand tons. This is a little less than half of what we have. The European Union has the largest gold stock, with approximately ten thousand tons. It is clear that the floating-rate fiat system is chaotic as well as unstable. There are five ways country's use to weaken their currencies:

1. Lower interest rates

2. Quantitative easing

3. Selling your own currency for other currencies, causing your currency to flounder

4. Talking down the value of your currency publicly (This what the Fed does from time to time)—making hints to discourage speculation from betting on strength—deceiving the people

5. As a last resort, using protectionism tariffs, embargoes, and other barriers to free trade. These can be used to offset the benefits of an enemy's devaluation.

In his book, *The Economic Consequences of the Peace,* John Maynard Keynes' cites Vladimir Ilyich Lenin's speech with regard to destroying capitalism, In it, Lenin stated "that the best way to destroy the capitalistic system was to debauch the currency. There is no subtler, no surer means of overturning the existing basis of society than to debauch the currency in a manner which not one man in a million is able to diagnose."

What Lenin was talking about was the illusion of money. For example, John and Mary earn $100,000 per year. We have 3 percent inflation. John and Mary receive a 2 percent raise. What did they gain? They lost approximately $1,060 in purchasing power due to inflation!

Chapter 3

A GOLD STANDARD FOR THE TWENTY-FIRST CENTURY FOR AMERICA AND THE WORLD

Article 1, section 8 of the Constitution states as follows: "To coin money, regulate the value thereof, and of foreign coin, and fix the Standard of Weights and Measures; To provide for the punishment of counterfeiting the Securities and current Coin of the United States."

I begin this chapter with Article 1, section 8 of the Constitution to make the point that our Founding Fathers wanted honest and stable money to be the foundation of a dynamic and growing economy. Although gold and silver were not mentioned, only coins, paper money was not mentioned either.

When the Continental Congress made the decision to fight Britain for our independence, they created the Continental dollar, which was not backed by gold.

The story of the Continental dollar may or may not be familiar to you. Each colony was permitted to print as many dollars as it wanted. When we won the Revolutionary War, we experienced hyperinflation. The Continental dollar was retired between 1779–1790. The Idaho Observer quotes Thomas Jefferson who said, "Everyone through whose hands a bill passed, lost on that bill what it lost in value during the time it was in his hands. This was a real tax on him, and in this way the people of the United

States actually contributed those millions of dollars during the war and by a mode of taxation the most oppressive of all the most unequal of all."

During the colonial period, we were on the gold standard. Gold and silver coins were circulated. People would deposit their gold and silver coins in the bank. The bank would issue a receipt, paper money, which we still use today. During colonial times, one ounce of gold equaled one dollar. When people saw that prices were going up, they exchanged their paper notes for gold and silver coins. By engaging in this practice, inflation was kept at a bare minimum.

Prior to 1837, the United States was on and off the gold standard. In 1837, President Andrew Jackson vetoed a bill presented to him by Congress. This bill called for the renewal of the charter for the second central bank, called the Bank of the United States. President Jackson vetoed the bill, because he believed in the gold standard. His veto was sustained by one vote.

The record of stability under the classical gold standard from 1837 to 1862 and from 1870 to 1913 is without parallel. Consumer prices varied in a 26 percent range in those sixty-two years and stood at almost the same levels at the beginning and end of both periods. Average inflation was one-tenth of one percent, while the average annual variation of prices in either direction was 2.2 percent. From 1879 to 1913, when the United States and other countries were on the gold standard, US prices ranged only 17 percent. Average inflation was only one-tenth of one percent, while the average variation of prices in either direction was 1.3 percent. This is in contrast to the average price variations during and after the Civil War, when we went off the gold standard.

Under the gold standard, all international transactions were done in gold. Gold is neither friend or foe. Gold is neutral and keeps us honest. When J. P. Morgan appeared before Congress in 1912, he said, "Gold is money. Everything else is credit."

For the sixty-two years that we were on the gold standard, one dollar purchased $100 worth of goods and services.

When a country has stable and trustworthy money, people tend to save more. Other countries will invest in countries with a stable country. Money always goes where it is treated the best. The pillar of prosperity is a stable currency with stable purchasing power.

When we decided to go back on the gold standard in 1837, we followed the lead of our British cousins. Great Britain had gone back on the gold standard in 1717. For over two hundred years, 3.89 British pounds equaled one ounce of gold. Lenders had the confidence that they would be paid back in money that would not lose its value. Capital investments in Great Britain exploded. The strength of Britain's currency helped create capital markets that turned Britain into the world's most powerful nation. With most of the world on the gold standard, more wealth was created in the 1800s than in all previous centuries combined.

Keynesians and monetarists focus too much on supply of money rather than demand. If the demand is not there, an attempt to create money sets up what in the 1930s was called "pushing on a string." The economy cannot grow without increases in productivity, coupled with low taxes, minimal regulations, tort reform, good education, and modern infrastructure.

Trust is not the only reason that we need currency stability. Stability is essential if money is to fulfill its role as an instrument of communication in the marketplace. The great Austrian School economist Friedrich von Hayek explained that money facilitates communication in the market, and in society, through the mechanism of prices. When money is made artificially unstable by government, the information it provides ends up being corrupted. Both producers and consumers respond to distorted market signals. The end result is gluts, shortages, or market bubbles.

As a standard of measurement, an instrument of communication, and a promoter of trust, money facilitates the creation of wealth in a society. Money is not wealth; it is simply a tool. Adam Smith defined money as an instrument of commerce and a measure of value.

In his book *Reviving America*, Steve Forbes said,

> Sound money via the gold standard would mean that median incomes would once again rise in real terms. When you have fiat money, prices go up and salaries go down. We get money that is devalued and purchases less and less goods and services. A gold standard would significantly reduce inflation. From 1821 to 1914 the cost of living in Great Britain went up 0.1 percent a year. Compare that to the double digit rate of inflation in the United States between 1971 when the last link to gold was severed, until 1983 when the bout with inflation was conquered.

Since 1983 the average rate of inflation has been 3 percent, based on a highly imperfect CPI calculation. A gallon of gas in the United States in 1971 was sixty cents a gallon. Before the collapse of energy prices, it was $3.50 per gallon.

Eliminating inflation is not the same as price stability. Prices under a gold standard will fluctuate due to the law of supply and demand, which is not to be tampered with.

Market distortions are created by inflation because people could easily mistake a rise in prices due to an increase in demand when the reason is inflation caused by too much money chasing too few goods! Market distortions are also caused by excessive taxation and regulations.

Gold-based money, however, would enable the market system of communication to convey the true worth of goods and services being exchanged. In other words, price signals would be free of inflation. The gold standard will not eliminate the business cycle. It will mitigate the business cycle. Since I believe in the Austrian School of economics, the business cycle is a natural cause of events. If we combined the gold standard with a flat income tax and minimal regulations, instead of boom and bust, we would go to an ebb and flow. Our recessions would be short and shallow as long as individuals and businesses had significant capital at their disposal. If we can make this happen, and I know that we can, we can keep layoffs at a minimum during mild recessions. In a true free-market economy, recessions should be viewed as a time out. There will always be over speculation, and there will always be people who overborrow. When the market sees mal-investment, it should take a time out and clear itself of these problems.

The great Austrian School economist Ludwig von Mises diagnosed the problem of booms and busts in the 1920s. The root cause of bubbles is excessive credit expansion, which originates at the central bank! In his book the Theory of the Business Cycle, Ludwig Van Mises wrote, "There is no means of avoiding the final collapse of a boom brought about by credit expansion. The alternative is only whether the crisis should come sooner as a result of a voluntary abandonment of further credit expansion or later as a final and total catastrophe of the currency system involved."

Every American student must take courses in finance in order to learn how markets work! You can teach someone to read a chart and a graph and so on. Everything in this life is timing. The right time to start a business is when the yield curve is upward sloping, which signals the beginning of a recovery. Prospective new business people should also look at the labor participation rate.

The first turning point of suspending the gold standard came in 1914, which marked the start of World War I.

On June 28, 1914, a Serbian named Gavido Princep assassinated King Ferdinand, the head of the Austria-Hungarian Empire. On July 18, 1914, Austria-Hungary declared war on Serbia. Europe immediately went off the gold standard. Britain and the United States stayed on the gold standard. We were able to do this because we entered the war in 1917 (the same year of the Bolshevik Revolution) and fought for only one year. The Bolsheviks had an easy time overthrowing the czar because Russia was suffering from hyperinflation. An armistice was signed in 1918.

The second tuning point occurred at the council of Genoa, in 1922 when the finance ministers of the world met in Genoa, Italy. At the time of the conference, our Federal Reserve bank was only eight years old. The gold exchange standard was not a pure gold standard of the type that existed from 1870 to 1913. It was a hybrid in which both gold and foreign exchanges, principally US dollars, UK pound sterling, and French francs, could serve as reserves and be used for settlement of any balance of payments. After the First World War, citizens in most major economies no longer carried gold coins, as had been common prior to 1914.

In theory, a country's foreign exchange reserves were redeemable into gold when the holder presented them to the issuing country. Citizens were free to own gold. International redemptions were meant to be infrequent, and physical gold possession by citizens was limited to large bars, which are unsuitable for day-to-day transactions. The idea behind this proposal was to have a gold standard but have as little gold as possible in circulation. The gold that was available was to remain in vaults at the Federal Reserve Bank of New York, the Bank of England, and the Banque de France, while citizens grew accustomed to using paper notes instead of demanding bullion. The gold exchange standard was, at best, a poor imitation of a true gold standard and, at its worst, a fraud. In one of his articles, the author of *Currency Wars*, *The Death of Money*, and *The New Case for Gold*, James Rickards stated the following:

> Most important, nations had to choose a conversion rate between their currencies and gold, then stick to that rate as the new system evolved. In view of the vast paper money supply increases that occurred during the first world war, most participating nations, chose a value for their currencies that was far below prewar rates. In effect, they devalued their currencies against gold and returned to a gold standard at the new lower exchange rate. France, Belgium, Italy and other members of what later became known as the gold bloc pursued this policy. The United States received large gold inflows during the war, and as a result, it had no difficulty maintaining gold's prewar 20.67 per ounce exchange rate. After the gold block devaluations, and with the United States not in distress,

the future success of the gold exchange standard now hinged on the determination of a conversion rate for UK pound sterling. The UK under the guidance of chancellor of the Exchequer, Winston Churchill, chose to return sterling to gold at the prewar equivalent to 3.89 pounds equals one ounce of gold.

Mr. Churchill felt duty bound to return the pound to its prewar parity so as to maintain London's standing as the world's financial center and this would also benefit British citizens and bondholders. His mistake was that he raised interest rates too much, which caused deflation that led to Britain falling into a depression in 1926. What is ironic is that, three years later (1929), our stock market crashed. The conventional wisdom at the time was that we were in a recession. The Federal Reserve at the time made the crucial mistake of raising interest rates when they should have been reduced. At a seminar with the late professor Milton Friedman, Mr. Bernanke acknowledged the error and apologized. He assured us that this serious mistake would never happen again. I will discuss QE in detail in the next chapter.

Jacques Rueff was President de Gaulle's chief economic advisor and head of the French Central Bank. Dr. Rueff was one of the most respected economists in the world.

The following is from the testimony given by Dr. Lewis Lehrman before congressional Subcommittee on Domestic Monetary Policy & Technology on the gold standard.

> "No less ominously, on the eve the Great War, the gold standard, the gyroscope of the Industrial Revolution, the proven guarantor of one hundred years of price stability, the common currency of the world trading system. The monetary standard of commercial civilization -- was suspended by the belligerents.
>
> The Age of Inflation was upon us.

The overthrow of the historic gold standard, led during the next decade to the great inflation of France, Germany and Russia. The ensuing inflationary convulsions of the social order, the rise of the speculator class, the obliteration of the savings of the laboring and middle classes led directly to the rise of Bolshevism, Fascism, and Nazism -- linked, as they were, to floating European currencies, perennial budgetary and balance of payments deficits, central bank money printing, currency wars and the neo-mercantilism they engendered.

Today, one observes -- at home and abroad -- the fluctuations of the floating dollar, the unpredictable effects of its variations, the new mercantilism it has engendered, and the abject failure to rehabilitate the dollar's declining reputation. Strange it is that an unhinged token, the paper dollar, is now the monetary standard of the most scientifically advanced global economy the world has ever known.

The insidious destruction of the historic gold dollar -- born with the American republic – got underway gradually, in the 1920s, during the inter-war experiment with the gold-exchange standard and the dollar's new official reserve currency role. It must be remembered that World War I had caused the price level almost to double. But after the war, Britain and America tried to maintain the pre-war dollar-gold, sterling-gold parities. Designed at the Genoa Convention of 1922, the official reserve currency roles of the convertible pound and dollar collapsed after 1929 in the Great Depression -- a collapse which helped to cause and to intensify the worldwide deflation and depression"

They failed and the world was sentenced to inflation. The argument that the anti-gold inflationist people make is that there is not enough gold in the world. This argument is nonsense. It's not the quantity of gold, but the price that a future gold commission would set it at. During the sixty-two years that we were on the gold standard, we only backed up the money supply up to 40 percent with gold. The result was inflation at one-tenth of 1 percent. According to an article written by James Rickards, if we achieve 40 percent gold backing of the money supply, gold would have to be $10,000 per ounce.

Mr. Rickards goes on to say, "In other words, a certain amount of gold can always support any amount of money supply if its price is set properly." I would point out that Nevada has gold that has yet to be mined.

All impediments to the granting of permits to mine gold must be removed. There is a gold mine located in the western part of Alaska. This mine is not in production due to the EPA! I will comment further on regulations in the final chapter.

As I am studying this discipline, I have come to the conclusion that there will be another financial crisis that will lead to a complete loss of confidence in paper money around the world. There is also growing dissatisfaction with central banks around the world. This will lead to either the elimination of central banking or the reform of central banking worldwide.

In my view, the reason we did not go back to the classical gold standard after World War I was because central banking was in its infancy. The third central bank, The Federal Reserve was only eight years old. Governments liked the idea of controlling the money supply. When you control the money supply, you control the economy! This is why the involved governments made up the excuse that the world did not have enough gold. That excuse was false. It was about the never-ending quest for more power! There were gold discoveries in the Yukon in Canada and throughout the world.

I would ask you to contemplate the following: Gentlemen, during the course of your lives, did you have to take on a second job to meet your monthly obligations? Ladies, did you have to go out to work part time or full time when you would have rather stayed home and raised your children full time! Have you ever felt that you have made these many sacrifices, but you still are not getting ahead? If you have any of these feelings, it isn't your fault. The fault lies with the government for not seeing the evil of fiat money and what it has done to families throughout many generations!

I am sure that we can agree that children need three things when they are being raised: love, discipline, and stability. It is the youth of America who have suffered because of currency devaluation!

I am of the opinion that a gold commission must be appointed by the next president. I suggest that Dr. Ron Paul and Dr. Lewis Lehrman be appointed as co-chairpersons. I am confident that they will appoint the best economists from the Van Mises Institute who would set the right price for gold. In order to go back on the gold standard, the budget must be put on the path to balance. The gold commission should decide whether or not a central bank is needed. What should be taken into consideration is the harm that they have caused to our economy!

My own view is that the central bank should not control interest rates or the money supply. The amount of money that should be in the system should be determined by the law of supply and demand. Money is a commodity and should be treated as such. The most important price signal is the short-term money market rate. This signal is the determining factor in deciding how much money should be in the system. The Treasury should print the money and not the Fed!

The Humphrey-Hawkins Full Employment Act, which was signed into law by President Carter in 1978, should be repealed. This law gave the Fed a dual mandate. This law mandated that the Fed should also target unemployment. The only way a central bank can do that is by lowering interest rates and printing more money. This is another example of Congress abrogating its responsibilities under the Constitution.

Throughout history, economies grow. They contract and evolve due to new technologies. These challenges must be addressed by the executive and legislative branches of government at the federal, state, and local levels.

The former and late distinguished Congressman Carter Glass coauthored the Federal Reserve Act. What he envisaged was a bank of last resort, in other words, a banker's bank. If a bank got into trouble with nonperforming loans, the Federal Reserve would loan money to the bank. He never contemplated that the central bank would engage in open market operations (buying and selling government debt). The intent of the new system was to provide liquidity to business and industry through a process called "rediscounting." The twelve Federal Reserve Banks would provide cash advances to local government banks. The commercial banking system would be backstopped by a reliable source of cash to meet unexpected depositor withdrawals, which would eliminate the need for banks to call in business loans and disrupt the flow of commerce.

Congressman's Glass's concern was that banks would forward earnings to Wall Street banks, which would subject this money to speculation. The decentralized Federal Reserve system was designed to have banks deposit their excesses to the Federal Reserve banks for safekeeping. When a bank goes to the Fed as a lender of last resort, the Fed by law must charge a penalty rate equal to 1 percent above the rate offered by the ten-year Treasury note, which is the benchmark for interest rates around the world. The days of public bailouts must come to an end. Part of the Fed's new responsibilities is to conduct stress tests for its member banks. The Fed must be audited once a year by an independent auditing firm appointed by the finance committee in Congress.

They should also decide how much debt to GDP we can handle, given our past economic performance. In my view it should be no more than 60 percent. In order for there to be sustained economic growth, our GDP growth per year must always be ahead of the debt. The same principle holds true for businesses and families! I would also suggest that they come up with the best methodology for calculating inflation, which should include food and energy!

In order to have the world join us, we need an international conference to decide the three Ps—purchase power parity. The best way to do this in my view is to take an average of the exchange rates for each country over a five- or ten-year period. I believe this method is the most suitable, because to judge a currency's performance in the foreign-exchange market would not be accurate enough to accomplish what we want, which is one exchange rate for all participating nations. The forex market is known for its volatility. All countries who participate in the gold standard would be on the same rate of exchange. All countries' currencies will be backed by gold up to 40 percent of the money supply, which was the case from 1870 to 1913. Being on one exchange rate will be advantageous to our exporters, because they would not have to deal with floating exchange rates. As previously mentioned, no nation can devalue its currency, since gold cannot be devalued. What this would come down to is honest and fair competition: who makes the best cars, construction equipment, etc. That is the way it should be. Honest and ethical competition brings out the best in all of us. This is the first step to world peace.

If we really trusted fiat money, why would there be hedges against inflation? The hedges against inflation are gold, real estate, and fine art. The working poor cannot afford any of those three. The middle class can afford, at this time, to buy gold as long as it remains relatively inexpensive. They can also afford to buy real estate. We have billions of dollars invested in hedge funds. If we were on the gold standard, these hedge funds would not be necessary. That money could be put to work in opening new businesses and expanding existing ones. Since World War II, we have had recessions every six years. In a recessionary cycle, investors always turn to commodities, specifically gold. In our hearts of hearts, we have always trusted old reliable.

Chapter 4

THERE IS NO RECOVERY

We have all heard the word "bubble" discussed by TV commentators. No one bothers to define the term. We are also living in a bubble economy. I would like to offer a definition of a bubble and a bubble economy. This definition is taken from a series of books titled *Aftershock*, written by Robert Wiedemer, David Wiedemer, and Cindy Spitzer.

> A bubble is defined as an asset value that temporarily booms and eventually busts, based on changing investor psychology, rather than underlying, fundamental economic drivers that are sustainable over time.
>
> A bubble economy is an economy that grows in a virtuous upward spiral of multiple rising bubbles. Real estate, stocks, private, debt, the dollar and government debt that interact to drive each other up and that will eventually fall in a vicious downward spiral as each falling bubble puts downward pressure on the rest, eventually pulling the whole economy down.

Since the start of the QE program, we have lost an additional 26 percent of our purchasing power. The money supply has been increased by 400 percent. However, the velocity of money, which is the amount of times money changes hands, shows a downward trend since the start of QE in 2008. The labor participation rate at the beginning of QE was approximately 66 percent. The labor participation rate has shown a downward trend since the start of QE in 2008. The labor participation rate is arrived at by dividing the total number of people who are not working and who have given up looking for a job into the total number of people who are working. It is impossible to have a 5 percent unemployment rate under these conditions. According to John Williams of ShadowStats.com, the true unemployment rate is approximately 22.9 percent and holding.

The jobs that the president alleges to have created are mostly part-time jobs in the discretionary spending sector of our economy.

QE has failed. QE was nothing more than a backdoor bailout of Wall Street and the federal government. The Fed can print money, but it cannot force people to spend money or force banks to loan money. Keeping interest rates at such low levels has enabled the federal government to continue with its irresponsible borrowing and spending. As a result of this irresponsibility, we lost our triple-A credit rating. The loss of our triple-A credit rating is serious. However, it has had no effect on Congress's or the president's behavior. At the time of the crisis, Congress tried to put the blame of the loss of our triple-A rating on the rating agencies. This is simply not the case. Irresponsible spending and borrowing were the root causes.

A credit rating is something that we earn by responsible handling of finance! When Pierre Trudeau was the prime minister of Canada. Canada lost its triple-A credit rating due to socialist policies adopted by the prime minister. It took Canada seven years to regain their triple-A rating. We can only regain our triple-A rating by showing our foreign and domestic creditors that we are finally getting serious about reducing our debt and putting our budget on the path to balance.

The interest on the national debt as of today is approximately $250 billion a year. If nothing is done, the interest on the debt alone will continue to eat away at important parts of our budget. We are in uncharted waters. Keeping interest rates at such abnormally low levels has resulted in a loss of $8 trillion of interest payments on our passbook savings accounts, money market funds, and certificates of deposits. Penalizing savers, like inflation, is legalized theft! These low interest rates have forced investors to take their capital overseas in search of higher yields. Money always goes where it is treated the best. These abnormally low interest rates have put pension funds and Insurance companies in a bind. Pension funds and Insurance companies as a matter of practice invest heavily in our bond market and other bond markets throughout the world.

I spent forty years in the insurance business. If I sold you a fixed income annuity, guaranteeing you 3 percent interest on your money for the life of the annuity, I am contractually obligated to do so. If I cannot get 3 percent in our bond market, I am forced to take the money overseas. My company's charter does not permit me to invest in the junk bond market. It is too risky. Since bond markets and banks overseas have negative interest rates, I am forced to put money in our stock market.

The people at the Fed are very smart people. They knew what the ramifications of their policies would be. Mr. Bernanke wanted to boost stock market prices. We all want the stock market to go up. But the stock market must go up for the right reasons: increasing revenue and profits. Markets are places where honest and ethical price discovery is found. The Fed's QE policy has practically destroyed honest and ethical price discovery. There is a complete disconnect between stock valuations and the real economy. The Case-Shiller PE ratio was conceived by Robert Shiller of Yale University. This ratio is based on average-inflation adjusted earnings of the S&P 500 from the previous ten years, taking inflation into account. The mean average as of July 8, 2016, was 16.68. The stock market valuation as of the same date was 26.45. It is obvious that the stock market is overvalued and will correct again. There always was and there will always be a moral hazard to cheap money. This excessive credit expansion was created by the Federal Reserve. It is about time that they be held accountable.

After exploding five times between 1987 and 2008, household debt temporarily went flat. Consumers did reduce their debt by $400 billion, or 3 percent lower than it was since 2008. Net business investment from 2009 to 2015, was $562 billion, which was lower than what it was in the year 2000. What has gone unreported is that there is an auto loan subprime crisis. Car loans have been extended to five years. The auto finance companies and probably some banks have granted loans with no money down. Based on a report done by Stanberry Associates, the defaults are beginning to happen.

Once again, it has been proven that no central bank can know what people and businesses are going to do with their money. It is none of their business. QE1 was necessary. QE2 and QE3 were not.

In his thesis, titled *The General Theory of Employment and Money*. John Maynard Keynes, who I am no fan of, defined a recession/depression as follows: "A chronic condition of subnormal activity for a considerable period of without any marked tendency either toward recovery or toward complete collapse. A cyclical downturn is viewed as temporary, a phase that can be remedied with spending of the classic Keynesian kind. A structural downturn, by contrast is embedded and lasts indefinitely unless adjustments in key factors are made. These factors are labor costs, labor mobility, taxes, regulations, and other public policies are made."

If we apply this definition to our economic performance from 2009 to the first quarter of 2015, our economic growth averaged only 2 percent. There is no economic recovery!

By pretending that the problem is not structural, Congress and the Fed conveniently avoided making structural changes.

The problems in our economy are structural, not cyclical. The structural problems are fiat money, excessive taxation, regulation, litigation, subpar education, and infrastructure neglect. There is only one way for an economy to grow, increasing productivity, which is accomplished through the creation of new businesses, expansion of existing ones, and invention of new technologies. One of the best periods for increasing productivity was in the 1950s and 1960s. During this period, for every dollar that the federal government borrowed, we received 2.41 in economic and productivity growth. During 1970s, due to double-digit inflation, we only received fifty cents of economic and productivity growth for every dollar borrowed.

Today, after $800 billion dollars borrowed, we have only received three cents in economic and productivity growth on the dollar.

Labor productivity, which measures an industry's total output divided by the hours worked by its employees, ticked up 2.6 percent in the wholesale trade sector, 1.9 percent in retail trade and only 0.3 percent in food services and drinking places, according to an article in New York News and World Report in August 2016, "between 1987 and 2012, productivity expanded each year at an average rate of 3.1 percent in wholesale trade, 2.8 percent in retail trade, and 0.4 percent in food and drinking places. That means all three sectors detailed in the latest report showed below-trend gains."

In his blog, former budget director David Stockman made the following comments on productivity:

> The US working age population between 16 and 65 totals 205 million, meaning that on a standard work year basis of 2000 hours, the potential labor force amounts to 410 billion hours. However, according to the BLS own data, only 230 billion labor hours are currently being utilized by the US economy from the potential hour's pool. So all things being equal the unemployment rate is actually 44 percent. The point, of course, is that virtually everything which impacts the 180-billion-hour gap between potential and actual hours employed is beyond the reach of monetary policy, for instance, about 18 billion hours are removed from productive employment by social security disability recipients and 40 billion potential labor hours are unavailable owing to young adults enrolled in higher education. Yet neither of these represent unchanging natural rates of unavailable labor supply. In fact, they are heavily impacted by public policies originating outside of the central bank, and which can change significantly over modest periods of time. For instance, the ratio of disabled workers to the population aged 16-65 rose from 2.82 percent in 2000 to 4.34 percent at present. That gain is

primarily due to the relaxation of eligibility standards for qualification in such areas as back pain and bureaucratic drift toward higher rates of favorable case determinations. Thus at the 2000 disability ratio of 2.82 percent there would currently be 5.8 million workers on the rolls or 11.5 billion unavailable labor hours. That compares to the actual level of 9 million workers on disability and 1.8 billion unavailable hours. Needless to say, in the scheme of things the 6.5 billion hours lost to higher disability rates is not a trivial difference. It represents the equivalent of 3.7 million nonfarm payroll jobs. That's more new jobs than have been celebrated on jobs Friday for the last 18 months running.

The story is similar with the 40 billion labor hours not available owing to the 20 million students enrolled in higher education. In this case, the enrollment rate for the prime student age population [18-24] has risen from 35.5 percent in 2000 to about 40.5 percent at present. Yet it is surely the case that liberalization of the Pell Grant program and the eruption of student debt outstanding from about 150 billion to 1.3 trillion during the last 15 years has had a powerful impact on that gain. Accordingly, a reasonable estimate is that the massive ratcheting up of state aid for higher education has caused a minimum of 4 billion labor hours to exit the jobs market.

Moreover, that begs the question as to the appropriateness and efficacy of the underlying public policy bias in favor of massive state support for 4-year higher education. Arguably, one-third or more of college students would be better served by on the job vocational training.

I agree with the distinguished David Stockman. The unanswered question is why have we neglected vocational schools? There will always be a need for electricians, HVAC mechanics, plumbers, carpenters, steamfitters, bricklayers, etc. These are the people who built America. They are America's forgotten people. We have a power grid that is vulnerable to cyberattack. Our power grid needs to be modernized! Do we have enough electricians to do the work? Our roads and bridges are in disrepair due to neglect. Where are the workers going to come from? The new workers should be American workers, not foreigners! The so-called brilliant geniuses in Washington haven't figured this out. The reason being is that they do not use common sense.

In his book *The Theory of the Business Cycle*, the great Austrian School economist Ludwig Van Mises, in describing productivity, used a stream of water as an analogy. The stream of production must flow unimpaired from the time the raw material is purchased to the time that the final product is presented for sale. Our productivity stream is interrupted by the payroll tax, which is 12.4 percent of the first $113,700. We had a payroll tax holiday two or three years ago. At that time, the salary cap was $106,700. Congress pulled another fast one. The government admits that the payroll tax is the most regressive of all taxes. This is due to the fact that it increases the cost of labor. Two-thirds of all inputs that go into productivity is labor. Throughout history, it has been proven that productivity and innovation are the principal drivers of economic growth. Even though the payroll tax funds Social Security, we can eliminate the payroll tax and replace it with a 10 percent consumption tax, excluding housing. This would reduce the cost of labor by 12.4 percent and encourage people to start new businesses, which our country desperately needs. I understand that the minimum wage must be increased, but not to $15 per hour! It should go up gradually to $9 per hour. The way to solve the problem of the minimum wage is to teach a skill. This can be accomplished by opening more vocational schools!

Ever since President Nixon cut the dollar's last link to gold, we have experienced moderate to high inflation. The 1970s was known as the period of stagflation, also known as the "misery index." We had 13 percent interest rates with 15 percent inflation. Our interest rates were minus-2. There is a difference between the nominal interest rate and the real interest rate. The nominal rate is the rate quoted before taking inflation into account. You subtract the inflation rate from the nominal rate and you get the real interest rate. This is the rate that should be quoted.

After we went off the gold standard, the booms and busts that followed have gotten worse. During the boom period, especially when interest rates are at very low levels, there is an overinvestment in the capital goods part of our economy (e.g., heavy construction equipment, cars, and heavy machinery). During the boom period, people tend to take on too much debt. When the bust comes, which is beginning now, people start to sell other assets to pay off their debts. These assets depending on the debt level of a company or the individual is sold at fire-sale prices. This process spreads like a contagion. This is the process that economists call "bad deflation."

There are deflationary pressures not only in our economy, but also in the world economy as well. The central banks and the governments are afraid of bad deflation. In a bad-deflation environment, prices go down, and the purchasing power of the dollar rises as well as the value of the debt. Deflation also destroys government tax collections. If a worker makes $100,000 per year and gets a $10,000 raise when prices are constant, that worker has a 10 percent increase in his or her standard of living. The problem is that the government takes $3,000 of the increase in taxes, so the worker only gets a $7,000 raise. If a worker gets no raise and prices drop 10 percent, the worker gets a ten percent increase in his or her standard of living, because of the reduction in prices. The people keep the gain because the government has no way of taxing the benefits of deflation.

The central bank and the government want increases in spending. They will not get it, because people are too indebted. The market must be allowed to clear itself of its mal-investments. The way to accelerate this process is to cut taxes and spending simultaneously. This will result in an orderly and responsible transfer of wealth from the government that took it to the people who have worked and sacrificed all their lives to earn it.

There is also good deflation. Good deflation appeared in our economy at the start of the Industrial Revolution. As we learned to do more with less, prices eventually went down and then leveled off due to supply and demand. This has nothing to do with gold. Prices under the gold standard will fluctuate, due to supply and demand. What is just as important is that under the gold standard, purchasing power will increase, and the dollar will purchase more goods and services. This is the equivalent of a raise.

I would ask that you consider the fact that since we went off the gold standard, we introduced hedge funds, which are designed to hedge against inflation. They are gold, real estate, and fine art. Working poor people cannot for the most part afford these hedges. Most middle-class people can afford gold and real estate. Eventually, they may not be able to afford gold because the price of gold will go much higher.

Since World War II, we have had recessions every six years. And during these recessions, we have always turned to old reliable gold. In our hearts of hearts, we know that fiat money cannot be trusted. Now it is time for all of us Americans to admit the truth.

Chapter 5

KEYNESIAN THEORY VS. THE AUSTRIAN SCHOOL OF ECONOMICS

In 1936 John Maynard Keynes wrote his thesis, *The General Theory of Employment, Interest, and Money*.

At the time of the Great Depression in the 1930s, economists were unable to explain the cause of the Great Depression. Keynes overturned the prevailing idea that free markets would provide full employment. The intent was that anyone who wanted a job would have one.

Keynes asserted that aggregate demand, which is measured by the sum of spending of households, businesses, and the government, is the most driving force in the economy. Keynes argument that a lack of aggregate demand would cause prolonged periods of unemployment. He stated that a country's output is the sum of consumption (government and consumer spending and investment) and exports. During a recession/depression, demand goes down. This results in reduced investment by business.

Keynes favored countercyclical policies to boost aggregate demand. These policies called for deficit spending and inflation. In order to control inflation, the currency is devalued, which results in a loss of purchasing power. This evil policy falls the hardest on the working poor and middle class, who can least afford to bear the loss of dollar purchasing power. Keynes especially favored labor-intensive infrastructure projects to stimulate employment and stabilize wages during recessionary periods. Keynes also believed that a reduction of interest rates would also act as a stimulus so that business would be encouraged to take on additional debt so as to expand their businesses. Keynes believed in short-term solutions to economic problems. He once said, "In the long run, we are all dead." Keynesian policy was popular until the 1970s when we incurred stagflation, which is minimal growth and high inflation. Keynes's theory became unpopular because it had no appropriate policy response for stagflation.

Monetary economists doubted that government's ability to regulate the business cycle.

They believe that a responsible use of monetary policy (reducing interest rates) can have a positive effect on the economy in the short run. However, the monetarist school believed that increasing the money would cause inflation in the intermediate term. Keynesians did accept this critique.

Keynes also believed that these activist policies would reduce the amplitude of the business cycle. I believe that Keynes' assertion is wrong. This assertion was made in Keynes' thesis, The General Theory of Employment, Interest and Money.

Excessive government spending has led us down the path of budget deficits, as far as the eye can see, and excessive debt, which is the rope that we have around our necks, that is preventing GDP growth.

There is only one way to grow our economy: produce, consume, and save the balance. As previously mentioned, productivity comes from starting new businesses and expanding existing ones. This is how we built America.

It is morally wrong to pass on this excessive and irresponsible debt to future generations. Part of the principles of our country is to leave future generations with a legacy of wealth, not a legacy of debt.

I hope that the next president will recognize this and call for an international conference and begin discussions on debt reduction to a more manageable level. According to an article written by David Stockman in his Blog the

Contra Corner, total debt by all countries is approximately $225 trillion. This is a world gone mad.

I am of the opinion that all student debt should be forgiven in exchange for four years of service to our country. This can be accomplished by serving in the military, doing volunteer work for your place of worship, working as a volunteer in a not-for-profit hospital, or in the community by teaching a young poor child how to read.

Volunteerism is the thousand points of light that President George H. W. Bush spoke about.

The Austrian School of Economics

The Austrian School of economics is a school of economic thought that is based on the concept of methodological individualism, that social phenomena result from the motivations and actions of individuals. This theory originated in the late-nineteenth- and early-twentieth-century Vienna with the work of Carl Menger, Eugen Bohm, Von Bawerk, Friedrich von Weiser, and others. It was methodologically opposed to Prussian Historical School. Current-day economists working in this tradition are located in many different countries, but their work is still referred to as "Austrian economics."

Among the theoretical contributions of the early years of the Austrian School are the subjective theory of value, marginalism in price theory, and the formulation of the economic calculation problem, each of which has become an accepted part of mainstream economics. Many economists are critical of the current-day Austrian School and consider its rejection of econometrics and aggregate analysis to be outside of mainstream economic theory. The Austrian School theorizes that the subjective choices of individuals, including individual knowledge, time, expectation, and other subjective factors, cause all economic phenomena. Austrians seek to understand the economy by examining the social ramifications of individual choice, an approach called "methodological individualism." It differs from other schools of economic thought, which have focused on aggregate variables, equilibrium analysis, and societal groups rather than individuals.

In the twentieth and twenty-first centuries, economists with a methodological lineage to the early Austrian School developed many diverse approaches and theoretical orientations.

In 1949, Ludwig von Mises organized his version of the subjectivist approach, which he called "praxeology." Praxeology is the study of those aspects of human action that can be grasped a priori. In other words, it is concerned with the conceptual analysis and logical implications of preference, choice, means and schemes, and so forth. In his book *Human Action*, Mises stated that praxeology could be used to deduce a priori theoretical economic truths and that deductive economic thought experiments could yield conclusions that follow irrefutably from the underlying assumptions. He wrote that conclusions could not be inferred from empirical observation or statistical analysis and argued against the use of probabilities in economic models.

In the twentieth century, various Austrians incorporated models and mathematics into their analyses. Austrian economist Steven Horwitz argued, in 2000, that Austrian methodology is consistent with macroeconomics and that Austrian macroeconomics can be expressed in terms of microeconomic foundations.

Fundamental Tenets of the Austrian School

1. Methodological individualism: In the explanation of economic phenomena, we have to go back to the actions or inaction of individuals; groups or collectives cannot act except through the actions of individual members.

2. Methodological subjectivism: In the explanation of economic phenomena, we have to go back to judgments and choices made by individuals on the basis of whatever knowledge they have or believe to have and whatever expectations they entertain regarding

external developments and, especially, the perceived consequences of their own intended actions.

3. Tastes and preferences: Subjective valuations of goods and services determine the demand for them so that their prices are influences by actual and potential consumers.

4. Opportunity costs: The costs with which producers and other economic actors calculate reflect the alternative opportunities that must be foregone; as productive services are employed for one purpose, all alternative uses have to be sacrificed.

5. Marginalism: In all economic designs, the values, costs, revenues, productivity, etc. are determined by the significance of the last unit added or subtracted from the total.

6. Time structure of production and consumption: Decisions to save reflect time preferences regarding consumption in the immediate, distant, or indefinite future, and investments are made in view of larger outputs expected to be obtained if more time-taking production processes are undertaken.

7. Consumer sovereignty: The influence consumers have on the effective demand for goods and services and through the prices that result in free, competitive markets, on the production plans of producers and investors, is not merely a hard fact but also an important objective, attainable only by complete avoidance of governmental interference with the markets and restrictions on the freedom of sellers and buyers to follow their own judgment regarding quantities, qualities, and prices of products and services.

8. Political individualism: Only when individuals are given full economic freedom will it be possible to secure political and moral freedom. Restrictions on economic freedom lead, sooner or later, to an extension of the coercive activities of the state into the political domain, undermining and eventually destroying the

essential individual liberties that capitalistic societies were able to attain in the nineteenth century.

Opportunity Cost: The opportunity cost doctrine was first explicitly formulated by the Austrian economist Friedrich von Wieser in the late nineteenth century. Opportunity cost is the cost of any activity measured in terms of the value of the next-best alternative foregone (that is not chosen). It is the sacrifice related to the second-best choice available to someone, or group, who has picked among several mutually exclusive choices. Opportunity cost is a key concept in mainstream economics and has been described as expressing the basic relationship between scarcity and choice. The notion of opportunity cost plays a crucial part in ensuring that resources are used efficiently.

Capital and Interest: The Austrian theory of capital and interest was first developed by Eugen Bohm von Bawerk, supply and demand. He stated that interest rates and profits are determined by two factors: supply and demand in the market for final goods and time preference.

Bohm von Bawerk's theory was a response to Marx's labor theory of value and capital. Bohm von Bawerk's attacked the viability of the labor theory of value in the light of the transformation problem. His conception of interest countered Marx's exploitation theory. Marx famously argued that capitalists exploit workers by paying them less than the fruits of their labor sell for. Bohm-Bawerk countered this assertion by invoking the concept of time preference to demonstrate that everyone values present consumption more than future consumption and, therefore, that a difference between the smaller salary laborers are paid in the present and the greater price for which the goods they produce are later sold need not be exploitive.

Inflation: In Mises's definition, inflation is an increase in the supply of money.

Mises went on to say, "In theoretical investigation there is only one meaning that can rationally be attached to the expression inflation: An increase in the quantity of money in the broader sense of the term, so as to include fiduciary media as well, that is not offset by a corresponding increase in the need for money again in the broader term, so that a fall in the objective exchange-value of money must occur."

Hayek pointed out that inflationary stimulation exploits the lag between an increase in money supply and the consequent increase in the prices of goods and services. And since any inflation, however modest at first, can help employment only so for any length of time only while it accelerates. Mild steady inflation cannot help; it can lead only to outright inflation. That inflation at a constant rate soon ceases to have any stimulating effect and, in the end, merely leaves us with a backlog of delayed adaptations, is the conclusive argument against the mild inflation represented as beneficial even in standard economic textbooks.

Austrian theory emphasizes the organizing power of markets. Hayek stated that market prices reflect information, the totality of which is not known to any single individual, which determines the allocation of resources in an economy. Because socialist systems lack individual choices, individuals act on their personal information. Hayek argued that socialist economic planners lack all of the knowledge required to make optimal decisions. Those who agree with this criticism view it as a refutation of socialism, showing that socialism is not a viable or sustainable form of economic organization. The debate rose to prominence in the 1920s and 1930s, and that specific period of the debate has come to be known by historians of economic thought as the "socialist calculation debate."

Mises argued in a 1920 essay, "Economic Calculation in the Socialist Commonwealth," that the pricing systems in socialist economies were necessarily deficient because if government owned the means of production, then no prices could be obtained for capital goods as they were merely internal transfers of goods in a socialist system and not objects of exchange, unlike final goods. Therefore, they were unpriced, and hence, the system would be necessarily inefficient since the central planners would not know how to allocate the available resources efficiently. Rational economic activity is impossible in a socialist commonwealth.

Business Cycles: The Austrian theory of the business cycle focuses on banks' issuance of credit as the cause of economic fluctuations. Although later elaborated by Hayek and others, the theory was first set forth by Mises, who believed that banks extend credit at artificially low interest rates, causing businesses to invest in relatively roundabout production processes. Mises stated that this led to a misallocation of resources, which he called "mal-investment."

According to the theory, mal-investment is induced by banks' excessive and unsustainable expansion of credit to businesses. Businesses borrow at unsustainable, low interest rates and overinvest in capital-intensive production processes, which in turn leads to a diversion of investment from consumer goods industries to capital goods industries. Austrians contend that this shift is unsustainable and must eventually be reversed, and that the readjustment process will be more violent and disruptive the longer the putative mal-investment in capital goods industries continues.

Ludwig Van Mises writes in his book *Theory of Money and Credit* that, "There is no means of avoiding the final collapse of a boom brought about by credit expansion. The alternative is only whether the crisis should come sooner as the result of a voluntary abandonment of further credit expansion or later as a final and total catastrophe of the currency system involved."

According to the Austrian view, the proportion of income allocated to consumption rather than saving is determined by the interest rate and people's time preference, which is the degree to which they prefer present to future satisfactions. According to this view, the pure interest rate is determined by the time preferences of the individuals in society. If the market rate of interest offered by banks is set lower than this, business borrowing will be excessive and will be allocated to mal-investment.

As previously mentioned in another chapter, we have had a recession every six years since the end of World War II. What studies have shown is that there was, for the most part, an overinvestment in capital goods. In our recessions, it is the capital goods sector of the economy that always gets hurt the worst. This is due to the high unit cost of autos, construction equipment, etc. Overinvestment leads to excessive inventories that have to be marked down, which leads to loss of profits.

A split with regard to Austrian school thought surfaced in the 1940s. The group that identifies itself with Mises and Rothbard believe in strict laissez-faire thought. Both Mises and Rothbard viewed central banking as dangerous and too controlling. They believed, as I do, that interest rates should be determined by the markets, since they are our most important price signal. The amount of money that should be in the system at any one time should be determined by market forces. It is the money market interest rate that is our most important price signal.

Van Hyack and his followers believe that a central bank is essential. The Hyack group is more accepting of government intervention.

It is a well-known fact that the Federal Reserve has engaged in central planning since they opened for business in November of 1914. The Fed influences short-term money market rates, because it controls the Fed fund rate, which is the rate that the Fed charges banks for overnight loans. The banks should negotiate the overnight rate among themselves. The Fed should have no control over interest rates.

Under a market system, the market will decide how much money should be in the system at any one time. Throughout history, it has been proven that a free market without cronyism is the best allocator of resources. The money market interest rate is our best pricing signal. In his book *Reviving America*, Steve Forbes proposed that the Fed be audited once a year.

In 1978, President Carter signed the Humphrey-Hawkins Act. This law gave the Fed the dual mandate to track and ensure full employment. The Fed can only accomplish this by reducing interest rates and printing money. This act gave the Fed control over the economy with the exception of taxes and other regulations! The structural problems in our economy need to be addressed by the executive and legislative branches at all levels, federal, state, and local! This is another example of Congress abrogating its responsibility under the Constitution! This law should be repealed. The Fed (if it is decided that we need it) should be limited to bank supervision and the lender of last resort. If banks need an emergency loan, they should be charged a penalty rate equal to the interest rate on the ten-year Treasury note, which is the benchmark interest rate for the world.

Economics is the study of the allocation of scarce resources. It is also the study of human behavior. We have the best technical tools to assist us in spotting trends in various asset classes. In order for us to be better people and, by extension, have a better country, we need to always be in touch with our human natures. One of the weaknesses of our human nature is the normalcy bias. There are times in our respective lives when we find it difficult to face the truth. The signs were there that there was a problem with subprime mortgages; these signs were ignored by the Fed. Mr. Bernanke stated that the subprime problem was contained. Nothing could be further from the truth. The Fed are poor forecasters. The reason for this is the Fed and other economists use the equilibrium theory.

The equilibrium theory is based on the false assumption that the economy works like a clock that needs rewinding or resetting. When the economy is out of equilibrium, policy makers think that if they apply the right doses of fiscal and monetary policy, the economy will fall back into equilibrium. This assumption is false. Markets are complex systems capable of producing highly surprising outcomes. Markets can be, at times, inefficient in the sense of ignoring value for extended periods of time. For example, there is a complete disconnect between the value of stocks and price. The cause of this is excessive liquidity (cheap money).

The right methodology to use is the Bayesian technique, which is used by our intelligence agencies. Complexity theory tells us that the next financial panic will be far worse than those that have gone on before. This is due to the enormous size of the financial system. Causal inference teaches us that events are path dependent. This means that the next event in a sequence depends in part on the one that came before. In other words, past history is taken into consideration. The Bayesian model does not tell us what will happen. It tells you what might happen. Most importantly, it has intermediary events, which intelligence analysts call "indications" and "warnings." For example, since the recession of 2008, commercial banks have grown by 25 percent. The amount of derivative trading has also increased. Nothing has been done to date with regard to reforming derivative trading. Fifty percent of the nation's wealth is concentrated in five banks. This is not good risk management, this is insanity. Therefore, the chances of a severe banking crisis have risen. The right thing to do is break up the banks, as Jim Rickards suggests, and limit derivative trading. There are 310 million people that reside in our country. All lives matter. The economic wellbeing of 310 million people must come first.

The Austrian School of economics is compatible with our way of life. Our Constitution is based on individual rights and freedom. The Austrian School emphasizes entrepreneurship and the expansion of wealth, which can only come from a good education. As mentioned earlier, increases in productivity are the principal drivers of economic growth. When we started to build our country in the late 1700s and 1800s, we produced, we consumed, and we saved the balance. We must be courageous enough and humble enough to acknowledge our mistakes and resolve to correct them. The Austrian School of economics also calls for stable currencies linked to gold. They believe that a stable currency linked to gold will produce stable purchasing power and attract foreign investment. A currency represents three things to a country. It is the foundation upon which great and prosperous economies are built. A currency represents part of a country's sovereignty, and it is part of a country's identity.

When the world was on the gold standard from 1870–1913, there was peace in the world. Economies grew and prospered. There were no wars. I call these forty-three years the "golden years" in world history. Mankind can live in peace. We need to remove the obstacles to peace. Creating a gold standard for the twenty-first century and convincing the rest of the world to go along with it will be a major step toward bringing peace to our troubled world! When President Kennedy gave his speech, setting a goal that we put a man on the moon in ten years, he stated the following: "We do the hard things, not because there hard, but because there right." Creating a gold standard for the twenty-first century and convincing the world to go along with us will be hard, but it is right!

Chapter 6

LIES AND STATISTICS

When President Nixon was in office in the 1970s, he became concerned about the high inflation numbers. He called in the chairman of the Federal Reserve, Arthur Burns, to "review" the problem.

Chairman Burns came up with a concept called "core inflation." Core inflation includes all items offered for sale in the market, except the two necessities of life: food and energy. At the time, his argument was that food prices were too volatile due to weather conditions. Energy prices were too volatile due to geopolitical problems, especially in the Middle East. Chairman Burns had a point regarding energy, but not food. The world has changed. In my view, we are now an energy-independent nation. At the present time, the Commerce Department calculates the producer price index and excludes food and energy. and the Bureau of Labor statistics calculates inflation. They include some food items but exclude energy.

The BLS is responsible for tracking prices for thousands of items. These statistics should be as accurate as possible, since businesses use these statistics as a guide to make business decisions. If the methodology used is inaccurate, thousands of businesses could make serious mistakes, which cause the loss of millions of jobs.

In recent years, the BLS, with the approval of Congress, adopted a concept called "chained CPI." Under this methodology, if a price of a food product such as steak goes up too much, the BLS simply removes it from the food basket and uses a substitution: chop meat or chicken. This deceitful practice has resulted in the government understating inflation by as much as 50 percent.

In an article written on December 27, 2012, Charles Goyette stated, "Use of the chained CPI, moderating the reported rate at which prices are climbing, would result in almost 150 billion in reduced cost of living increases for recipients and other budget savings between 2014 and 2022. There are also elements of the tax code linked to the CPI, including personal exemptions, standard deductions, and limitations on retirement accounts. Implementing the chained CPI would increase tax revenue by 62 billion."

Instead of suppressing what is really taking place and making the necessary adjustments in an honest and straightforward manner, our government chooses to lie. There is no doubt in my mind that this is being done for political reasons.

Mr. Goyette goes on to say, "During the Reagan administration, when housing prices were running up, the Bureau of Labor Statistics altered the way it calculated housing's contribution to the CPI. In 1983, the bureau began calculating the housing portion of the CPI by using an owner's equivalent of rent. It began estimating how much a homeowner would get if he rented his house out. It was a change that massively understated the real increase in the cost of living during the real estate bubble years.

"Applying the CPI calculations that were used in the 1990s to price changes in late 2012 reveals price inflation running about 3–3.5 percent higher than the official numbers the government releases. Using the 1980 calculation, inflation today is running as much as 7 percent higher than the government reports."

The way to report increases in housing prices is to use the fair market value of commercial and residential real estate. This should be done by region. Another way of reporting price increases is to report the cost of building homes and commercial real estate. Residential and commercial real estate are insured based on the cost to rebuild residential and commercial real estate, less the foundation and land. This can also be done by region. Using either one of these methodologies would require more work. However, the price increases will would be based on the truth, not lies! According to ShadowStats.com, inflation (including food and energy) is approximately 3–7 percent higher than what is currently being reported. The federal government also uses the Hedonic method to calculate inflation. For example, if you receive a notice from your cell phone company that you are receiving a free app, the BLS credits inflation, because you are receiving more value for the amount paid. What the BLS doesn't do is debit inflation when the quality of a product goes down and we pay more for it. An example is furniture. Furniture is made out of pressboard. Lacquer is used to hide this. We have one currency—everything should be under one roof, the Treasury. The Treasury can create a division within itself to take on the responsibility of calculating inflation. When the next gold commission is appointed, one of their assignments should be to determine the most accurate way to calculate inflation. Inflation must always include food and energy. Honest statistics from the government are what we should demand. This is one of the ways that we will go about rebuilding the trust that has been lost.

In a speech given in 1966, former Fed chairman Alan Greenspan stated the following:

In the absence of the gold standard there is no way to protect savings from confiscation through inflation. There is no safe store of value. If there were, the government would have to make its holding illegal as was done in the case of gold. The financial policy of the welfare state requires that there is no way for the owners of wealth to protect themselves. This is the shabby secret of the welfare statists tirades against gold. Deficit spending is simply a scheme for the hidden confiscation of wealth. Gold stands in the way of this insidious process. It stands as a protector of property rights.

For twenty-seven years, Mr. Greenspan was our Fed chairman. He had the opportunity during his tenure to try and convince Congress and the presidents that he served under to put us back on the gold standard. The question that has never been asked of Mr. Greenspan is, why did you turn your back on your principles?

I am critical of the way the government reports unemployment. The Bureau of Labor statistics excludes people who are unemployed and whose benefits have expired. It appears that exclusion of this group would understate the true unemployment number.

This figure also does not tell us how many jobs are available but cannot be filled because our students do not have the skill set to fill these jobs.

The government defines underemployment as a person working part time that should be working full time. This definition is incomplete. Underemployment should also include those people who are working a full-time job outside their field of study. For example, if Mary or John obtained a master's degree in business marketing and are working as department managers in a department store, they are underemployed. Under this present system, we have no way of knowing where the strengths or weaknesses in our economy lie.

We would be better served if we broke the economy down into three broad categories: capital goods, discretionary spending, and staples. Every month we would know how many full-time and part-time employees were hired in each category. We would subtract the number of people that retired in each category. We would then have honest numbers to work with.

According to an article written by former budget director, David Stockman most of the jobs created in the private sector were in the discretionary sector. For example, part-time and full-time waiters and waitresses, bartenders, etc. As of today, we still do not know how many jobs are available that cannot be filled. This is unacceptable. This is no way to run a country.

Chapter 7

AMERICA'S FORGOTTEN DEPRESSION, LESSONS NOT LEARNED

In 1921 America sustained a depression. This depression lasted one year. Warren Harding was president. Calvin Coolidge was vice president. Herbert Hoover was Commerce secretary. Dr. Arthur Mellon was Treasury secretary. The information that I am about to share with you is taken from a book written by James Grant titled *The Forgotten Depression: 1921: The Crash That Cured Itself.*

President Harding succeeded Woodrow Wilson. The First World War started in 1914 as previously mentioned. From 1914–1916, we supplied our allies with weapons and war material. President Wilson had imposed a war tax and took over the railroads.

The following is a quote from the author, James Grant: "What can one say about the slump of 1921–22 and on the strength of which evidence can one say it. One can observe that the depression had a visible cause namely, the preceding inflation. Inflation distorts money, prices and values, but also the very architecture of an inflating economy."

The inflation of 1915–19 changed the way people invested, consumed, and planned. Rising prices invites speculation. Low interest rates and easy money emboldened the speculators. Easily accessible credit distorted the visible odds on success and failure alike. Businesses that may have gone under received a new lease on life. In the 1915–19 run up to the depression, the number of bankrupt business and the liabilities of those bankrupt, dropped to half of what had been before the war. Because 1919 had failed to deliver the wildly anticipated position depression, industrialists, banks, and farmers made plans for a still higher boom.

Certainly, many industrialists invested, some bankers loaned and most farmers planted as if inflation was in the offing. When those expectations collided with the facts of tight credit, high interest rates and falling prices, the industrialists, bankers and farmers recoiled.

Recorded business cycle historian, Wesley Class Mitchell, writing in the late 1920s, "Every price decline made the financial position of overexposed enterprises worse, reinforced the fears of insolvency and the pressure for liquidating indebtedness, this increased pressure for liquidating indebtedness, this increased the pressure to realize upon stocks of goods and so forced prices still lower."

By the contemporary reckoning of the English economist T. E. Gregory, "the world in 1921 was nearer to collapse than it has been at any time since the fall of the Roman Empire."

President Harding pointed out how tired the country was of progressive experimentation and great crusades. America's present need, he declared in May of 1920, the month before he was nominated, stated that the economy has to heal. "We do not need nostrums but normalcy, not revolution but restoration, not surgery but serenity."

President Harding went on to say, "The economic mechanism is intricate and its parts interdependent and has suffered great shocks and jars incident to abnormal demands, credit inflation and price upheavals."

War and the inflation induced by war finance had upset that mechanism and it fell to the people to fix it. "Prices must reflect the receding fever of war activities, he said, with a tip of the hat to the Federal Reserve's sponsored deflation. "Perhaps we shall never know the old level of wages, again because war invariably readjusts compensation. All the penalties will not be light or evenly distributed. There is no way of making it so. There is no instant step from disorder to order. We must face a condition of grim reality, charge off our losses and start a fresh is the oldest lesson of civilization."

In the fiscal year ending June 30, 1922, there was a reduction in federal outlays to $3.3 billion from $5.1 billion from the year before. This was done under the guidance of one of our greatest secretaries of the Treasury, Arthur Mellon. The budget had shown a $291-million-dollar surplus in fiscal 1920. The surplus increased under President Harding to $509 million in the depression year of 1921 and $736 million in the recovery year of 1922.

In a speech to a joint session of Congress on July 13, 1921, President Harding began by saying that the proposed bonus for veterans who served overseas was unaffordable. What the administration had come to understand during its four months in office was that conditions would stagger all of us were it not for our abiding faith in America. President Harding went on to request that taxes be reduced, refinance the war debts that our allies owed us.

"It is unthinkable," Harding continued, "to expect a business revival and the normal ways of peace while maintaining the excessive taxes of war. It is quite unthinkable to reduce our tax burden while committing our treasury to an additional obligation which ranges from 3 to 5 billion dollars." With regard to the expediency of printing more money, Harding reminded the senators of the constraints inherent in the gold standard. Our government must undertake no obligation which it does not intend to meet. No other government will pay our bills.

"We may rely on the sacrifices of patriotism in war, but today we face markets and the efforts of supply and demand and the inexorable laws of credit in time of peace."

What the uncounted millions of unemployed people needed was prosperity. Tax cuts and spending cuts would hasten prosperity. Stabilized finance and well-established confidence are both essential to restored industry and commerce.

The top marginal rate was reduced to 32 percent and the elimination of the excess profits war tax was abolished as of January 1, 1921. The corporate tax rate was raised 10 percent to 12.5 percent. The capital gains tax was initiated at 12.5 percent with no specific holding period. Surcharges on high earners (more than a million) was capped at 50 percent. President Harding had to compromise with regard to the mild tax increases in order to get Congress to postpone bonuses for our veterans. At this point, there was a consensus in Congress that raising taxes impaired economic growth. Both parties felt that the way to expand government revenue was more business startups. This meant that the proper economic incentives, low taxes and minimum regulations, should remain in place!

President Harding died in office in 1923. President Coolidge did not alter President Harding's policies. He won in a landslide in 1924. He won thirty-five states and 382 electoral votes. It was President Coolidge who once said, "America is about idealism; America is about business." We would be in far better shape if we had adhered to President Coolidge's words.

There were four phases to the Great Depression.

Phase 1: The Business Cycle

The depression of 1929 was not our first depression. It proved to be the longest and most severe. Several other depressions preceded it. Most other depressions lasted no more than two years. The previous depressions were largely due to incompetent government intervention, largely due to too much credit expansion.

Most monetary economists, particularly the Austrian School have observed the close relationship between increasing the money supply (credit expansion) and economic activity. When the government inflates the money supply, interest rates fall. This easy money as Ludwig von Mises has pointed leads to mal-investment. The cheap money is always invested in capital goods at the expense of consumer goods, which has occurred during QE! When the easy money effects on the economy mature and interest rates rise again, growth slows and the usual result is a recession. During the boom, prices rise as well as inflation. When interest rates rise, the money supply contracts. As mentioned previously bad deflation can and usually does ensue.

In his book, *America's Great Depression*, author and Austrian School economist Murray Rothbard documented that the Fed bloated the money supply by more than 60 percent from 1921 through mid-1929. Rothbard argued that this credit expansion (excessive money printing) drove interest rates down and pushed the stock market up to "dizzy heights" and gave birth to the Roaring Twenties. Other economists raised doubts that Fed action was as inflationary as Rothbard believed, pointing to relatively flat commodity and consumer prices in the 1920s as evidence that monetary policy was not so wildly irresponsible

Substantial cuts in high marginal income rates in the Coolidge years helped the economy grow. These tax cuts probably mitigated the effects of credit expansion. Tax reductions resulted in business expansion and increased productivity. The introduction of new technologies, which continued to teach us to do more with less, kept prices down.

The Fed began raising interest rates late in the 1920s. By 1928, the Fed was raising interest rates and reducing the money supply dramatically. The discount rate, which is the rate that the Fed charges member banks for loans, increased 4 times from 3.5 percent to 6 percent between January 1928 and August 1929. The Fed took further deflationary action by selling government bonds that they had purchased from their dealers for months after the stock market crashed. For the next three years, the money supply shrank by 30 percent. As prices fell throughout the economy, the Fed's higher interest-rate policy boosted real inflation adjusted rates dramatically. What the Fed should have done was to reduce interest rates after the crash, not continue to raise them.

In his book *A Monetary History of the United States, 1867–1960*, the late professor Milton Friedman and his associate Anna Schwartz argue conclusively that "contraction of the nation's money supply by one-third between August of 1929 to March 1933 was an enormous drag on the economy and largely the result of seismic incompetence by the Fed."

Phase 2

Contrary to public opinion, President Hoover started the new deal also known as government intervention. Against the advice of his Treasury secretary, Arthur Melon, President Hoover raised the top marginal tax rate to 63 percent, which choked off capital investment. As a side note, President Hoover was a geologist by education and a good businessman. He purchased a gold mine in Australia and turned a loss into a profit. He was a can-do type of man. When he was Commerce secretary, he helped charitable organizations raise money to help build temporary housing for the Mississippi flood victims of the 1927 Mississippi flood. He should be commended for his work as Commerce secretary. In contrast to President Harding and President Coolidge, who were more laid back, President Hoover's personality did not allow him to have the patience to sit back and allow the economy to heal itself.

The biggest mistake that Hoover made was the Smoot-Hawley Tariff, which essentially closed the door to foreign imports. As always, there was immediate retaliation, and the rest of the world sank into depression. Professor Barry Poulson describes the scope of Smoot Hawley:

> The act raised the rates on the entire range of dutiable commodities; for example, the average rate increased from 20 percent to 34 percent on agricultural products; from 36 percent to 47 percent on wines, spirits and beverages; from 50–60 percent on wool and woolen manufactures. In all, 887 tariffs were sharply increased and the act broadened the list of dutiable commodities to 3,218 items. A crucial part of the Smoot Hawley tariff was that many tariffs were for a specific amount of money rather than a percentage of

the price. As prices fell by half or more during the Great Depression the effective rate of these tariffs doubled, increasing the protection afforded under the act.

The Smoot-Hawley Tariff eventually lead to the Second World War.

Phase 3: The New Deal

President Roosevelt ran for president in 1932 and won by a landslide. He ran on a pro-business platform promising to lower taxes and balance the budget. He violated his party's plank and his promises to we the people. President Roosevelt immediately raised the top marginal rate to 79 percent. This choked off whatever was left of capital investment. He began his experiment with huge government intervention, which history shows failed miserably. In the first year of the New Deal, Roosevelt proposed spending $10 billion, while revenue was only 3 billion. Between 1933 and 1936, government spending rose by more than 83 percent.

As I mentioned in another chapter, President Roosevelt took us off the gold standard and confiscated gold from we the people. We were not allowed to own gold until it was demonetized in 1974. For forty-one years, we the people were denied owning real money, gold.

In a book by Lawrence Reed, *Great Myths of the Great Depression* he quotes from the diary of Treasury Secretary Morgenthau wrote, "If anybody ever knew how we really set the gold price through a combination of lucky numbers, I think they would be frightened." Roosevelt also single-handedly torpedoed the London Economic Conference in 1933, which was convened at the request of other major nations to bring down tariff rates and restore the gold standard. The reckless central bank had already destroyed the gold standard by the early 1930s. The elimination of the gold standard removed the impediment to excessive money printing and deficit spending, which we paid dearly for in later years. We the people needlessly suffered through a number of currency devaluations.

Frustrated and angry that Roosevelt had so quickly abandoned the platform on which he was elected, his budget director, Lewis Douglas, resigned after only serving one year.

During this phase, President Roosevelt tried to pack the Supreme Court, since the court declared a number of the agencies that he created unconstitutional. FDR talked Congress into passing the Social Security Act in 1935. As we know, Social Security is financed by the payroll tax, which is the most regressive tax that we have. He also got the minimum wage law passed. Although he receives credit for these two laws, the minimum-wage law prices unskilled workers out of the market, especially minorities.

Phase 4

The passage of the Wagner Act revolutionized American labor relations. It took labor disputes out of the courts of law and brought them under a newly created Federal Agency, the National Labor Relations Board, which became prosecutor, judge, and jury, all in one. Labor union sympathizers on the board further perverted this law, which already afforded legal immunities and privileges to labor unions. We abandoned a great achievement, equality under the law. The Wagner Act was passed in reaction to the Supreme Court's voidance of NRA and its labor codes. It aimed at crushing all employers' resistance to labor unions. Anything an employer might do in self-defense became an "unfair labor practice," punishable by the board. The law not only obliged employers to deal and bargain with the unions designated as the employees' representative, but also later board decisions made it invalid to resist the demands of labor union leaders. Armed with these new powers, labor unions went on a militant organizing frenzy. Threats, boycotts, strikes, seizures of plants, and widespread violence pushed productivity lower. It also increased unemployment. Membership in labor unions rose dramatically.

Historian William E. Leuchtenburg, no friend of free enterprise observed, "Property minded citizens were scared by the seizure of factories, incensed when strikers interfered with the malls, vexed by the intimidation of non-unionists, alarmed by flying squadrons of workers who marched, or threatened to march, from city to city." This created an unfriendly climate for business. Unreasonable union demands, coupled with high taxation, regulation, and excessive litigation, has caused businesses to move overseas. The country loses when this happens. In recent years, union membership has declined. Every state should be a right-to-work state. There should be no forced unionization. Part of our liberties is freedom of association, the freedom to associate with whomever we wish.

The root cause of the Great Depression was excessive credit expansion created by the Fed, which caused bubbles that eventually burst. Cheap money always invites excessive speculation. The Smoot-Hawley Tariff and tax increases by Hoover and Roosevelt only prolonged the agony. Unfortunately, and sadly, we still have not learned from the mistakes of the past. I attribute this to arrogance on the part of the government and the Federal Reserve.

Chapter 8

SDRS AND DERIVATIVES

The SDR is a new kind of money printed by the IMF. The idea was that it could be used as a reserve currency side by side with the dollar. This meant that if the United States cured its trade deficit, and supplied fewer dollars to the world, any shortfall in reserves could be made up by SDRs. The SDR is backed by nothing. The dollar, British pound, euro, and yen are used to calculate the value of the SDR. The breakdown is as follows: euro 37.4 percent, yen 9.4 percent, pound sterling 11.3 percent, US dollar 41.9 percent. This "world reserve currency" was to be used only in an emergency. The SDR would not circulate among populations. It would only be used in a financial crisis to settle international transactions.

The first issuance of SDRs occurred in 1970–72, during the period of high inflation, which was due to President Nixon closing the gold window. The IMF's first issuance totaled SDR 9.3 billion. The second issuance was from 1979–1981, consisting of SDR 12.1 billion. There was a thirty-year gap before the third issuance of SDRs. The third issue amounted to SDR 161.2 billion and a special issue of SDR 21.5 billion in August and September 2009, respectively. The total amount of issuance to date is $280 billion.

The problem with SDRs is that, once in circulation, they are inflationary. Once this money is put into circulation, it will cause inflation. As of today, because of our failed political system, we are still running huge trade deficits with the world, and we still have huge budget deficits. In a previous chapter, I quoted Dr. Lewis Lehrman and John Mueller, who explained the fiat reserve currency curse. In the same article, Dr. Lehrman and John Mueller went on to say,

> We hold our wealth in one of three forms: money, goods (including services) or securities, which are in effect claims on future goods. It is therefore a fundamental truth of accounting that the net international payments for official reserves (money) current account (trade in goods and services) and private capital account (securities) must equal zero. That is a surplus or deficit in one account requires an offsetting surplus or deficit in the other two combined. Simply put, if you trade $100 in currency for $50 in goods and $50 in securities someone else has done the same thing. Payments have to balance out. When foreign countries increase their dollar reserves, it means that US residents have bought much more foreign wealth than they have sold. The result is a net outflow of capital known as hot money because it is highly mobile, speculative, and very sensitive to fluctuations in interest and exchange rates."

The overall US balance of payments system has been running huge deficits since the 1960s and is getting worse.

Our trade deficit with China, according to Mr. Trump, is over $500 billion. We have a $58-billion trade deficit with Mexico. The answer is not excessive tariffs or currency devaluation, but hard bargaining. As previously mentioned, currency wars and trade wars are zero-sum games. It is we the people who end up losing.

Dollars held in reserve by foreign governments count. To assume that they don't assumes a closed world economy.

My concern about the IMF is that it is an international organization that is accountable to no one. We and other nations provide funding for the IMF. The same is true for the World Bank and the Bank of International

Settlements. What we must also be aware of that if these organizations gain too much power, our sovereignty could be put in danger!

Derivatives allow risk about the value of the underlying asset to be transferred from one party to another. For example, a wheat farmer and a miller could sign a futures contract to exchange a specified amount of cash for a specified amount of wheat in the future. Both parties have reduced a future risk: for the wheat farmer, the uncertainty of the price, and for the miller, the availability of wheat. However, there is still the risk that no wheat will be available due to causes unspecified in the contract. Although a third party, called a clearing house, insures a futures contract, not all derivatives are insured against counterparty risk.

From another perspective, the farmer and the miller both reduce a risk and acquire a risk when they sign the futures contract. The farmer reduces the risk that the price of wheat will fall below the price specified in the contract and acquires the risk that the price of wheat will rise above the price specified in the contract, thereby losing additional income that he could he have earned. The miller, on the other hand, acquires the risk that the price of wheat will fall below the price specified in the contract, thereby paying more in the future than he otherwise would and reducing the risk that that the price of wheat will rise above the price specified in the contract. In this sense, one party is the insurer for one type of risk, and the counterparty is the insurer for another type of risk.

Derivatives can be used to acquire risk, rather than to insure or hedge against risk. Thus, some individuals and institutions will enter into derivative contracts to speculate on the value of the underlying asset, betting that the party seeking insurance will be wrong about the future value of the underlying asset. Speculators will want to be able to buy an asset in the future at a low price according to a derivative when the future market price is high, or sell an asset in the future at a high price according to a derivative contract when the future price is low.

Derivatives trade over the counter and through intermediaries.

Warren Buffet called derivatives "weapons of mass destruction." These instruments, with the exception of future contracts, are exceptionally risky. Derivative trading has increased since 2008. Total derivative exposure is over $500 trillion worldwide.

Derivatives should not be used by pension funds, insurance companies, or municipalities. In the 1990s, Orange County, California, which is an upscale community in Southern California, had a $1-billion surplus. One bad derivative trade brought Orange County from surplus to bankruptcy. The economic wellbeing of thousands of lives was impacted. This madness and irresponsibility in our society must stop, if we are to save the country we all love.

The forex market is the largest market in the world. Every day, $4 trillion of currency exchange hands. Currencies are sold in pairs, for example, Euro/US, USD/JPY. When one currency goes up, the other must come down. This methodology is called "cross rates." At the Bretton Woods Conference, countries from around the world met to manage international trade. This established a forex system that relied on fixed exchange rates and formalized the dollar as the world's reserve currency.

As previously mentioned, President Nixon closed the gold window. The result was an international system in which the market set the value of a nation's currency, known as the floating rate system. This would become known as the forex market, but central banks and large international institutions previously dominated the market.

In recent years, the forex market has been opened up to individual traders. Now it seems that most forex trading is speculative, with hedge funds and institutional traders chasing profits around the world. Only a small percentage of market activity represents the traditional currency conversion needs of governments and large companies.

Major pairs include any combination of the US dollar, euro, Japanese yen, British pound, Swiss franc, and Canadian, Australian, and New Zealand dollars.

This market is volatile. I would caution the inexperienced investor not to invest in it. If you were contemplating investing in a foreign currency, I would suggest that you take courses in finance first.

The Bank of International Settlements is based in Basel, Switzerland. It was created in 1930. This organization is known as the central bank of all central banks. Over the years, it has served many functions. Its first function was to manage the $30 billion in reparations that the Germans had to pay after World War I. Over the years, they have run seminars and created suggested regulations for banks, known as Basil I–III. Top-secret meetings are held at this institution frequently. These meetings are held in secret with no accountability! To the best of my knowledge, our banks are complying with Basel regulations. We are smart enough to regulate our own banks—why the need for a foreign institution to offer suggested regulations? Our liberties are on a slippery slope without us realizing it! This is the primary reason for writing this book.

Chapter 9

PARTING THOUGHTS AND SUGGESTIONS

The Democrats and their allies in the media have misrepresented the Reagan record. The Democrats had control of the House of Representatives and the Republicans had control of the Senate for six out of the eight years of the Reagan presidency.

When President Reagan took office, we had the misery index, double-digit inflation, and high interest rates. Paul Volcker was chairman of the Federal Reserve.

The first law that President Reagan got passed was the Kemp-Roth tax cut bill. This bill reduced the top marginal rate from 70 percent to 50 percent. President Reagan along with Chairman Volcker were very concerned about the double-digit inflation of 15 percent, and they wanted it eliminated. In his book *Money Mischief,* the late professor Milton Friedman in his discussion of inflation stated, "The cure for inflation is just as bad as the disease itself."

In order to get inflation out of the system, Chairman Volcker had to raise the Fed funds rate to 20 percent before inflation was significantly reduced to under 4 percent. He combined the raising of the Fed funds rate with open market operations, selling government securities. To put it another way, the chairman had to deflate, "reducing the money supply," to accomplish this. This necessary medicine caused the recession of 1982.

To the best of my knowledge these two policy tools, raising the Fed fund rate and open market operations, are the only tools available to the Fed if this should happen again.

There was light at the end of the tunnel. We had seven uninterrupted years of growth that created over 17 million jobs. Our economy grew between 3–4 percent per year for seven straight years, without a recession. Every time there is a transfer of wealth from the government that took it, we have GDP growth! Decrease in taxes do not cause deficits—irresponsible government spending causes the deficits.

When we were growing up, we were lead to believe that when interest rates go up, it means that the economy is slowing down. False! Everything is relative. If interest rates are going up, the first question is how much? Rising interest rates can be a positive for our economy. It can mean that the market is signaling that it wants more money in the system and is willing to pay more interest to borrow it so that business owners can expand their businesses or start new businesses. Dr. Steve Sjuggerud is the author of a newsletter, *Daily Wealth*. He has studied rising interest rates. His study revealed that every time the Fed has been in a raising-rate cycle mode, stocks have gone up. Once again, ladies and gentlemen, we have been indoctrinated, not educated.

One of the first things President Reagan did when he took office was to appoint businessman, J. P. Peter Grace, who assembled a team of 168 business people to conduct the most extensive audit of the Federal government in our history. The Grace commission made over 2,100 recommendations on how to save money and reduce the size of the federal government. Congress refused to cut spending! In the last book that he wrote before he died, Mr. Grace forcefully argued that if all of those recommendations had been implemented, we could have saved approximately $450 billion over a five-year period. When you consider the fact that our economy was growing at 3.5 to 4 percent every year for seven straight years, President Reagan would have left us, at the least, with a balanced budget or, at the very best, a small surplus. Tax reform was passed in 1986, which helped our economy to continue to grow. Since no Republican candidate has ever adequately defended the Reagan record, I feel that it is time that the truth be told.

When our Founding Fathers met in Philadelphia in 1787, they hired three famous consultants to assist them in the drafting of our Constitution. They were Thomas Paine, Montesquieu, and John Locke. Thomas Paine wrote a book titled *Common Sense*, which is lacking in our leadership and in our population. This very important truth must be integrated in our daily discourse. Part of our problem is that these smug elitists come up with theories that do not work, for example, Keynesian economics. They lack the courage and humility to acknowledge, as I previously stated, that this economic theory, which prolonged the Depression, does not work. The use of this theory resulted in our borrowing $850 billion from generations who haven't yet been born. Every generation has a moral obligation to leave our country in a better financial position than we found it. This can only be done with better education, based on school choice. Education is a partnership between parents and the schools. It does not belong in the federal government. When I was growing up, we had parent-teacher associations.

Since we the people pay the bills through property taxes, we have the right to have a voice as to how our children are being taught and what they are being taught. The better the parental participation, the stronger the system will be. Common Core should be abolished as well as the Federal Department of Education.

Montesquieu was a Frenchman who came up with the concept of the separation of powers. Our Founding Fathers, who came from Puritan backgrounds, understood the strength and weaknesses of our human nature. By dividing the power of government, we the people have been protected for over two hundred years from tyranny!

John Locke, an English philosopher, agreed with the concept of separation of powers. Our system is breaking down. The culture war started in the 1960s. Our traditional values—a strong belief in God, faith, hope, and charity—is being challenged by the progressive left who believe in big government and socialism. This movement was started by Theodore Roosevelt. It is this expansion of government and regulations as well as central planning of our money supply that created the "deep state." Throughout world history, it was and still is the people of the world who create wealth. The governments throughout history take wealth through taxation and regulation.

Webster defines "socialism" as "a political and economic theory of social organization that advocates that the means of production, distribution, and exchange should be owned or regulated by the community as a whole."

Once the means of production are transferred to the community or government, we have central planning by governments, which includes regulations that are placed on business. This practice leads to tyranny. These regulations now total over $1.8 trillion. It is excessive taxation and regulation that are driving our businesses overseas. What the progressives do not understand is that money always goes where it is treated the best.

At the Constitutional Convention, our Founding Fathers were concerned about us taking on excessive debt. At the time of our revolution for independence from Britain, Britain and France were bitter enemies. The French loaned us substantial sums of money to finance the war. France is our oldest ally. Our first Treasury secretary, Alexander Hamilton, managed our finances. He pegged the dollar to gold at $19.69 per ounce. He created the bond market in order to pay off existing debt. He issued debt securities, Treasury bills, bonds, and notes that were sold to the public. The money raised would pay off existing debt.

The father of our Constitution, President James Madison, said the following about debt: "I go on the principle that a public debt is a public curse, and in a republican government, a greater curse than any other."

Thomas Jefferson: "We must not allow our rulers to load us with perpetual debt."

Alexander Hamilton: "Allow a government to decline paying debts and you overthrow all public morality."

George Washington: "Avoid occasions of expenses and avoid likewise the accumulation of debt."

Benjamin Franklin: "When you run in debt, you give power over your liberty."

Notes from *Liberty's Secrets: The Lost Wisdom of America's Founders* by Joshua Charles who quotes George Washington: "The preservation of the sacred fire of liberty, and the destiny of the republican model of government, are justly considered as deeply, perhaps as finally staked on the experiment entrusted to the hands of the American people. We either pass it on to our posterity as it was passed down to us, or it dies here and now. We either assume its risks and keep it, or eschew those risks and lose it forever. The choice is ours may we choose well."

We have chosen well up to the time of the progressive movement. The Progressives believe that the Constitution is an evolving document. It is no such thing. If our Founding Fathers intended that the Constitution be an evolving document, why would they write in a procedure to amend the Constitution, which is contained in Article V. In order to defeat the progressive movement, they must not be elected to public office.

To be fair and honest both political parties are responsible for the $20 trillion in debt. In the space of approximately forty years, we have gone from the world's largest creditor nation to the world's largest debtor nation. This can be accomplished by significantly reducing federal spending by bringing the federal government in compliance with the Constitution. In a previous chapter, I discussed this in detail.

In their book *Empire of Debt*, Bill Bonner and Addison Wiggin state the following about real wage increases.

1. Society must save money so that we have the capital to invest.

2. It must invest the savings in profitable businesses.

3. These capital investments must result in increased productivity.

The authors went on to say, "In the 25 years after World War 2, output per employee had risen at an average of 2.8 percent per year. During the 1980s this rate fell to 1.9 percent. There was a bump in productivity after 1995 but this was due to the Labor Department's new way of calculating it.

"National savings, excluding public savings, fell from 7.7 percent in the 1970s to only 3 percent by 1990. Business investment fell from 18.6 percent of GDP in the 1970s to 17.4 percent in the 1980s."

This was due to increases in regulation. President Reagan was only able to slow the increase in regulations down.

Bill Bonner and Addison Wiggin also listed the deceptions that our debt rests on.

1. That one generation can consume and stick the next generation with the bill

2. That you can get something for nothing

3. That the rest of the world will take Americas IOUs forever, no questions asked

4. That housing prices will go up forever

5. That American labor is inherently more valuable than foreign labor

6. That the American capitalist system is freer, more dynamic

7. That other countries want to be more like America, even if it is forced on them

8. That the virtues that made America rich and powerful are no longer required to keep it rich and powerful

9. That domestic savings and capital investment are no longer necessary

10. That the United States no longer needs to make things for export

As I previously stated in another chapter, the only way for an economy to grow is to increase productivity through business expansion and creating new businesses. There are two other aspects of economics that I would like to share with you. The first is the time value of money. No construction project in our country can start without a permit. The granting of permits is the responsibility of federal, state, and local governments. In his book *The Basics of Economics*, Dr. Thomas Sowell criticized governments for deliberately holding up permits for political reasons, incompetence, etc. Every day that a permit is delayed is a day of lost productivity, which translates into loss of income. We are wasting too much time. The permitting process must be streamlined at all levels of government. Ever since the beginning of QE, we have lost our focus on the most important part of economic growth!

The other aspect of economics is demographics. In an ideal economic situation, more children would be born every year than people retire. This is not the case anywhere in the world.

The birthrate in the United States dropped to a historic low in 2013. Some people say that this is a temporary setback and look for gains in jobs and wages to push fertility back up in future years. The absolute number of births fell by twenty thousand from 2012 to 2013, even as the number of women in their prime childbearing years 20–39 continued growing. The number of births per year per thousand women age, 15–44, fell to 62.5 in 2013. The fertility rate is a calculation of how many children a woman would have in a lifetime. According to an article written in *Forbes* magazine, the fertility rate is 1.87. When people write about fertility issues, they cite economic reasons, which is true. However, economics is a very general term. I am the oldest of four children. When I was growing up in the 1950s and 60s, the average family was six to eight people; husband and wife, four to six children. According to studies, the family unit has been reduced to two children and two parents. Unfortunately, due to the divorce rate, there are too many families without fathers. People that I have talked to state the reasons for not having more children is the cost of living. The reason for my writing this book is to focus on the core reason for our economic problems, currency devaluation due to the evil of fiat money. It is a shame that people who write about demographics do not zero in on the core problem. I hope that this book will be a step in the right direction.

The support system for productivity is our infrastructure which is in very poor condition due to neglect by politicians of both parties. In an article written by David Frazer in the *Financial Intelligence Report*, Mr. Frazer cites a study done by the American Society of Civil Engineers who gave a grade for each part of our infrastructure:

> Roads: Grade D. The amount of time we spend in the car is dead time. Productivity cannot take place. Estimated cost to address the problem, $170 billion per year.
>
> Bridges: Grade C+. There are 607,380 in our country; one in nine are structurally deficient. To bring bridges up to standard, we need to invest 20.5 billion annually.
>
> Transit: Grade D. It is estimated that deficient transit systems cost the economy $90 billion in 2010. Transit agencies throughout the country have experienced increase ridership and reduced funding.
>
> Aviation: Grade D: The FAA estimated that the cost of delays in 2012 was approximately $22 billion. The FAA estimates that the cost of congestion and delays to the economy will rise from $34 billion in 2020 to $63 billion by 2040.
>
> Ports: Grade C. Port authorities and the private sector are planning to spend $46 billion in capital improvements over the next number of years.

Inland waterways: Grade D-. This part of our infrastructure has not been updated since the 1950s. There is an average of 52 service interruptions a day throughout the system. Lost time equals loss of productivity!

Dams: Grade D. The average age of the eighty-four thousand dams is fifty-two years old. There are four thousand deficient dams that need to be upgraded. Estimated cost, $21 billion.

Drinking water: Grade D. "There are approximately 240,000 water main breaks in the United States every year." According to the ASCE, an investment of $21 billion will be required.

Hazardous Waste: Grade D. One in four Americans live within three miles of a hazardous-waste site.

Levees: Grade D–. There are one hundred thousand miles of levees throughout the country. Estimated cost, $100 billion dollars.

Wastewater: Grade D: Old pipes have to be replaced. Estimated cost of modernization, $298 billion over twenty years.

As I have said in other chapters, the money to address this neglect must come from savings that would be realized by reducing the size of the federal, state, and local governments, addressing our structural problems and focusing in on what makes economies grow: produce, consume, and save the balance.

Immigration: We are a nation of immigrants. It was legal immigration that made us a great country. My grandfather immigrated from Calabria, Italy, in the early 1900s. He manufactured shoes in Italy. He opened a shoe repair shop and bought the building and did very well for himself. When he immigrated, he had to have a sponsor and was examined upon entering the country at Governors Island in New York. He learned how to read and write English by reading the newspapers. He had to travel to work by public transportation. He knew when to get on and off by memorizing the color of the subway stations. I tell this short story to make a point that our immigration laws were stricter than they are today. Those laws were put in place to protect the population. Our immigration system is broken. What was once our greatest strength has turned into a weakness! The first line of defense of any sovereign country is its borders. We need to get control of our borders and begin deporting the illegal aliens who are in our jails. It costs us on average $32,268 per year to keep someone incarcerated.

It is bad enough that we have a million of our own citizens in jail. We do not need to be housing illegals. I am against amnesty. We need to start an orderly and responsible deportation process. We need to make a point to all nations that we are a nation of laws and principles. The people who are deported who wish to return will have to wait in line. We will allow those people who respected our laws to return first. The illegals must pay a fine for breaking our laws. Due to Obamacare, we are short approximately thirty thousand doctors. We need to get our priorities in order. American citizens must always come first. This is not isolationism; this is common sense.

One of the great saints of the Catholic Church, Saint Thomas Aquinas, had suggestions about immigration. Here they are.

St Thomas: "Man's relations with foreigners are twofold: peaceful and hostile; and in directing both kinds of relation, the law contained suitable precepts."

Commentary: "In making this affirmation, Saint Thomas affirms that not all immigrants are equal. Every nation has the right to decide which immigrants are beneficial, that is, peaceful to the common good. As a matter of self-defense, the state can reject those criminal elements, traitors, enemies, and others who it deems harmful or hostile to its citizens."

The second thing he affirms is that the manner of dealing with immigration is determined by law in the cases of both beneficial and hostile immigration. The state has the right and duty to apply its law.

Saint Thomas: "For the Jews were offered three opportunities of peaceful relations with foreigners. First, when foreigners passed through their land as travelers. Secondly, when they came to dwell in their land as newcomers. And in both these respects, the law made kind provision in its precepts, for it is written (Exodus22:21), "Thou shalt not molest a stranger (*advenam*), and again in Exodus 29, "Thou shalt not molest a stranger."

Commentary: "Here Saint Thomas acknowledges the fact that others will want to come to visit or even stay in the land for some time. Such foreigners deserved to be treated with charity, respect, and courtesy, which is due to any human of good will. In these cases, the law can and should protect foreigners from being badly treated or molested.

Saint Thomas: "Thirdly, when any foreigners wished to be admitted entirely to their fellowship and mode of worship. With regard to these ascertains, order was observed. For they were not at once admitted to citizenship; just as it was law with some nations that no one was deemed a citizen except after two or three generations, as the Philosopher says."

Commentary: "Saint Thomas recognizes that there will be those who will want to stay and become citizens of the lands they visit. However, he sets as the first condition for acceptance a desire to integrate fully into what would today be considered the culture and life of the nation.

"A second condition is that the granting of citizenship would not be immediate. The integration process takes time. People need to adapt themselves to the nation. He quotes the philosopher Aristotle as saying this process was once deemed to take two or three generations. Saint Thomas himself does not give a timeframe for this integration, but he does admit that it can take a long time."

Saint Thomas: "The reason for this was that if foreigners were allowed to meddle with the affairs of a nation as soon as they settled down in its midst, many dangers could occur, since the foreigners not yet having the common good firmly at heart might attempt something hurtful to the people."

Commentary: "The common sense of Saint Thomas is certainly not politically correct, but it is logical. The theologian notes that living in a nation is a complex thing. It takes time to know the issues affecting the nation. Those familiar with the long history of their nation are in best position to make the long-term decisions about its future. It is harmful and unjust to put the future of a place in the hands of those recently arrived, who, although through no fault of their own, have little idea of what is happening or has happened in the nation. Such a policy could lead to the destruction of the nation.

"As an illustration of this point, Saint Thomas later notes that the Jewish people did not treat all nations equally since those nations closer to them were more quickly integrated into the population than those who were not as close. Some hostile peoples were not to be admitted at all into full fellowship due to their enmity toward the Jewish people."

Saint Thomas: "Nevertheless it was possible by dispensation for a man to be admitted to citizenship on account of some act of virtue thus it is related (Judith14:6) that Achoir, the captain of the children of Ammon, was joined to the people of Israel, with all the succession of his kindred."

Commentary: "There were exceptions that were granted based on the circumstances. However, such exceptions were not arbitrary but always had in mind the common good. The example of Achoir describes the citizenship bestowed upon the captain and his children for the good services rendered to the nation."

The commentary was done by John Horvat who authored the book *Return to Order*. I highly recommend it. We need immigration reform. We should use Saint Thomas's suggestions as a guide for future legislation.

Race Relations: I was seventeen years old when President Johnson signed the 1964 civil rights bill. Race relations at that time were poor. I remember seeing segregated bathrooms while traveling with my family on a trip to Florida. Since that time, I believe that race relations have improved. More blacks own homes and businesses now than they did fifty-four years ago. Blacks dominate professional football and basketball and have made contributions in the area of music. There are more blacks on our police forces than fifty-four years ago. I see this as progress. Unfortunately, the media does not know the meaning of balanced reporting.

In 1968, the late Daniel Patrick Moynihan was assistant labor secretary under President Johnson. He became concerned over the deterioration of the black family. He issued what became the Moynihan Report.

Part of the report stated that the problem was the matriarchal structure of the black family. I cannot accept this part of the study. In my view, jobs were lost were due to jobs moving out of the inner city. The other problem is that these government programs created perverse incentives not to work. As I mentioned in other chapters, opening vocational schools is a big part of the solution. However, it must be understood that the motivation to better oneself must come from the mind and heart of the individual. The politicians, who for the most part are only interested in the next election, should be stressing this. Given our human nature, I find it very hard to believe that a black woman would not want a partner for life. We should always bear in mind that God created two genders to complement each other. Black women are no different than any other women of different races or cultures. I suggest that all citizens, especially African Americans, read the Moynihan Report.

The latest statistics of out-of-wedlock births in the United States as of 2012 is that 40.7 of all 2012 births were out of wedlock, which is appalling, and there are vast differences among racial and ethnic groups. Among non-Hispanic blacks, the number is 72.2 percent; for American Indians/Alaska Natives, it's 66.9 percent: 53.3 percent for Hispanics, 29.4 percent for non-Hispanic whites; 17.1 percent for Asian/Pacific islanders. It is impossible to break this vicious cycle of poverty if these out-of-wedlock births continue. As previously mentioned, the interest on our debt is $200 billion a year. These programs are becoming more and more unaffordable! We need real leaders who have the courage to confront the problem and say, in no uncertain terms, that this behavior is immoral and will not be accepted without consequence. If a man gets a girl pregnant, that individual will be legally liable for supporting the innocent child. It is time for tough love.

As we all know, the mainstream media has a liberal bias. Freedom of the press is one of our most cherished rights. But for every right that the Constitution safeguards, there is a correlative duty. The duty of the media is to provide unbiased reporting. Tough questions must be asked in the never-ending search for the truth. The media should be the guardians of the truth. We are all mortal. We make mistakes. When mistakes are made, they should be acknowledged and corrected, including an apology. What we have today is arrogance and corruption. The mainstream media has an open bias in favor of Democrats. By not exposing their mistakes, as they do to Republicans and other parties, they are doing a disservice to our country! We the people can fight back by not buying liberal publications and not watching them on TV. We must realize that we the people are part of a dynamic free market! We can and we should write letters to the sponsors of these programs, objecting to biased reporting. We should make clear that if sponsorship continues, we will purchase products from their competitors!

My fellow Americans, our traditional values have been under attack by the counterculture since the 1960s. We are losing this war because we have become too complacent! Remember that we the people, under our Constitution, are the employers, not the employees. We must reassert ourselves and fight for our rights. The liberal progressive movement must be defeated at all levels of government and never be elected to office again. Under the Declaration of Independence, our rights come from God—life, liberty, and the pursuit of happiness. Our Constitution guarantees an equal opportunity for all, free of discrimination. That is all we are owed. The freer we are from excessive taxation, regulation, and litigation, the better we will all be.

I hope that this book was informative.

Bibliography

Books

Bonner, Bill, and Addison Wiggin. *The New Empire of Debt*.
Casey, Doug. *Right on the Money*.
Charles, Joshua. *Liberty's Secrets*.
Davidson, James. *The Age of Deception*.
Forbes, Steve. *Reviving America*.
Forbes, Steve, and Elizabeth Ames. *Money*.
Friedman, Milton. *Money Mischief: Episodes in Monetary History*.
Grant, James. *The Forgotten Depression: 1921: The Crash That Cured Itself*.
Griffin, G. Edward. *The Creature from Jekyll Island*.
Hayek, Friedrich A. *A Tiger by the Tail*.
Katusa, Marin. *The Colder War*.
Kelly, Kel. *The Case for Legalizing Capitalism*.
Lehrman, Lewis. *Money, Gold, and History*.
Lehrman, Lewis. *The True Gold Standard*.
Monteith, Stanley. *Brotherhood of Darkness*.
Paul, Ron, *End the Fed*.
Paul, Ron. *Gold, Peace, and Prosperity: The Birth of a New Currency*.
Paul, Ron. *Pillars of Prosperity*.
Paul, Ron, and Lewis Lehrman. *The Case for Gold*.
Reinhart, C. M., and K. S. Rogoff. *This Time Is Different*.
Rickards, James. *Currency Wars: The Making of the Next Global Crisis*.
Rickards, James. *The Death of Money*.
Rickards, James. *The New Case for Gold*.
Rothbard, Murray N. *America's Great Depression*.
Rothbard, Murray N. *The Mystery of Banking*.

Skousen, Cleon. *The 5000 Year Leap.*
Sowell, Thomas. *Basic Economics: A Common Sense Guide to the Economy.*
Taylor, John. *First Principles: Five Keys to Restoring America's Prosperity.*
Von Mises, Ludwig. *The Theory of Money and Credit.*
Wiedemer, Robert. *Aftershock.*
Wiggin, Addison. *The Little Book of the Shrinking Dollar.*

Newsletters

Financial Intelligence Report: 888-766-7542
Stansberry Associates: 888-261-2693
Agora Financial: 800-708-1020

About the Author

Robert Calabro worked during his career in both retailing and insurance, and he has written The Great Betrayal in order to share with his fellow citizens what he has learned about monetary policy since retiring. His hope is that we will take our country back by following the Constitution and by harnessing the power of education. Robert currently lives in Brooklyn, New York.

www.ingramcontent.com/pod-product-compliance
Lightning Source LLC
Chambersburg PA
CBHW022118170526
45157CB00004B/1684